199 Ways To Improve Your Relationships, Marriage, And Sex Life

By L. B. Sommer

Copyright © 2012 L. B. Sommer

All rights reserved.

ISBN-10: 1479229415
ISBN-13: 978-1479229413

Dedication

I dedicate this book to divine love. I have loved and lost a few times in my life, but each time I have come away wiser, more determined to find true love. I guess that is why the Bible says love never fails. Even when the taste of love hurts, it makes our character stronger and leaves us longing for more. I hope and pray that an eternal divine love awaits me and everyone who reads this book.

Table of Contents

Foreword	Page 9
Chapter 1: 12 Basic Ways To Improve Any Relationship	Page 16
Chapter 2: 12 Basic Ways To Have A Successful Marriage	Page 30
Chapter 3: 50 Ways To Be A Better Mate	Page 44
Chapter 4: 40 Ways To Make Your Mate Feel Loved	Page 96
Chapter 5: 25 Ways To Avoid Unnecessary Conflicts	Page 138
Chapter 6: 20 Plus Ways To Resolve Differences Peacefully	Page 165
Chapter 7: 20 Ways To Re-vitalize A Relationship	Page 188
Chapter 8: 20 Ways To Improve Your Sex Life	Page 210
Chapter 9: The Keys To Happiness Are Within You	Page 232
Chapter 10: Meaningful Quotes About Life and Love	Page 245
Chapter 11: Funny Quotes About Relationships	Page 253
Disclaimer	Page 262

Foreword

I was motivated to write this book because I found a need for this type of information in my own life. Though as a child I was raised in a loving family, looking back now I must admit we were a completely dysfunctional family in many ways too. Since most of our skills and abilities in relationships are learned at a young age from our parents and our siblings, when I entered my first serious relationship I quickly realized how ill prepared and inept I was at being a good husband and father.

In my case, I did not have a Mother Teresa and a St. Peter for parents. My mother's own dysfunctional upbringing combined with a few of her own personal weaknesses and demons probably made her less than the ideal teacher of such skills. My mother had little time to teach us relationship skills as she was usually working one of her two full-time jobs while trying to raise five children as a single parent, My father's untimely death when I was a very young child also was a major factor in many ways to my own inadequacies and inabilities to be a stable and supportive partner. He was not there to teach me by example how to be a good man, good friend, or good father himself. Unfortunately these and many other factors contributed to me getting a late start in life on learning certain necessary relationship skills. Ultimately I entered my first two relationships totally unprepared and inept. Inevitably my first two serious relationships ended in failures. Thus I began a quest for self-improvement in hopes of ending my cycle of failed marriages.

Having officially graduated from the school of hard knocks, I could tell you I decided to write this book as my doctorate thesis for the fore mentioned school; however, that would be an exaggeration of fact and an extension of my B.S. degree (and I don't mean Bachelor of Science). The truth is that by writing this book I hope I can prevent others from encountering the same unnecessary heartaches I discovered in my own life. I sincerely hope I can share my lifetime of hard earned wisdom with others. I truly hope that the advice and suggestions that I accumulated in my own quest for self-improvement will help you find a peace and happiness in your own life, equal to what I eventually discovered in my own relationships.

I know from my own personal experiences that the advice and suggestions I offer in this book have benefited me and my relationships immeasurably. I never would have written this book if I did not strongly believe that this book would be of major benefit to others, such as you and your loved ones. Yet unfortunately, due to the realities of the legal world we live in, I find it necessary to write the following disclaimer. I hope that none of my readers will ever find the need to try to blame their own shortcomings or failed relationships on me.

DISCLAIMER: First and foremost, I want to state clearly that I am not a trained or licensed professional. I am not a trained or licensed doctor, psychologist, family counselor, or anything similar. Though I personally believe that the suggestions and advice I offer in this book can help the vast majority of my readers improve their own relationships, I make no claims or guarantees that the information provided in this book will be of any benefit to you and/or your relationships. I strongly recommend that anyone having serious issues in their own lives or relationships seek professional counseling whether it is from their own doctor, family therapist, psychologist, or a member of their religious community.

All the advice, information, techniques, suggestions and/or anything else that I offer in this book are provided for informational and entertainment purposes only. I would hope that through self-reflection and self-analysis my readers can determine for themselves which ideas and suggestions can improve their own specific circumstances and relationships. Though the advice I offer is usually supported by one or more so-called experts, I make no claims that any of my advice will be of benefit to you or your relationships specifically. I am providing this information to my readers with the expectation that my readers will be able to draw their own conclusions about which advice might be of benefit to themselves and their relationships. Since no two situations or relationships are the same, my readers must assume the responsibility for all consequences that occur by applying my advice to their own specific lives and circumstances. Again I strongly advise all my readers to consult with their own licensed and trained professional family counselor or doctor if they have any doubts about applying any of the techniques, information, and/or suggestions in this book to their own specific lives and relationships. Therefore the reader of this material must assume all responsibility for any decisions, actions, and/or non-actions they take or do not take in regards to ideas suggested in this book.

Chapter One: 12 Basic Ways To Improve Any Relationship

Be True to Yourself

BE YOURSELF!!! Don't try to be someone you're not. Your true colors will inevitably show in any long-term relationship, so it is best to be yourself right from the beginning. Any pretentious misrepresentation of yourself and/or your situation will be viewed quite negatively at best and as an outright lie to most at worst. Be honest, authentic, and sincere in all your relationships and dealings. Own your faults, admit your limitations, and communicate them clearly to your potential business partners, friends, and loved ones. If someone is incapable of accepting the real you then it is best for the relationship to end sooner than later. Why waste your time and energy building a relationship that is doomed to fail when your true nature is revealed later? If you show your best then do your worst others will be disappointed as they expect the first. However, if you show your worst but do your best then hopefully they will be impressed by your effort to make the relationship mutually satisfying and successful.

Follow the Golden Rule

Treat other people the same way you want to be treated. It is a simple rule that can solve all the world's problems and make everyone happy. It is definitely one of the most key elements in successful relationships. Human decency is actually a very contagious thing. It is very hard to return evil when offered only kindness. Think of the sweetest, most gentle person you know; now go try to be rude and crude to them deliberately, can you do it? I doubt it, unless you're a totally heartless person. Thus we need to treat others the way we want to be treated in all of our relationships so that can we can gain the respect, trust, and even the love of those we want to be closest to. A good partner is not self-centered; they understand that a relationship is a 50/50 preposition. A good partner realizes that what is invested into a relationship is often returned in kind. Treat someone right, and they will treat you right too.

Never Ever Lie

Everyone hates a liar, and everyone avoids a liar. This is why it is important to gain the respect and more importantly the trust of others by always telling the truth. Personal and business relations are always founded on trust and can only endure if that trust is not undermined by lies. Only an emotionally insecure person will start a relationship with a known liar, and only a fool will continue any type of relationship once a habitual liar has been exposed. Wise business-minded people will naturally avoid any substantial dealings with a known liar or make that person jump through numerous hoops to ensure that there is no deception involved in their dealings. Lies will usually cause other people to limit their relationship with you. On the other hand, the truth will always open doors and hearts. It will cause others to want to invest more with you, whether it is in a financial or in an emotional way. So never lie - especially to a friend, lover, or business associate.

Be a Good Listener

The art of listening is a life skill that everyone should be taught in school, but unfortunately we are not. A good listener will hear the spoken words AND what the person meant to say but did not say clearly for whatever reason. To be a good listener you must first be quiet and not interrupt when someone is speaking; you must hear every word that is spoken. Next, you must not be overly defensive or jump to conclusions too quickly. This is especially true when conversations are regarding conflict resolution or differences of opinion. Being understanding and agreeable will make conversations more productive, as others will be more willing to open up to you. After hearing someone's words, you must interpret objectively what was said and maybe even what was not said before responding appropriately. Remember a good listener should not be angered or challenged by what is said, as it is only the opinion of another person.

Control Your Tongue

"Death and life are in the power of your tongue." These inspired words will apply directly to the success and failure of all your relationships in life. A soft word at the right moment can diffuse a tense situation; a harsh word at the same moment can inflame it. Every word you speak is a choice you are making in regards to that relationship. Every word offered should be positive, encouraging, and constructive; this is what builds trust, respect, and even love. There is no room for negativity in any good relationship. Friendship, love, and business dealings all begin with the positive words we choose. The best advice I ever got in life came from my mother. She constantly told me throughout my childhood, "If you cannot say something nice, then don't say anything at all." This is excellent advice for any type of relationship. If you can learn to control your tongue, then you will able to control the outcome of most of your relationships.

Be a Positive Person

An optimistic outlook and attitude will create positive results in your life. Positivity starts in your mind, so be happy and have a "can do" attitude. Smiles are magnetic, so wear yours every day. There is no room for negativity in any relationship whether it is personal or business oriented. It is a well-known fact - people are naturally drawn to others who are habitually cheerful. People always shun negative individuals who bring them down in life; so think positively about your life, your work, your relationships, and most importantly your goals. Don't be a complainer or a whiner. Don't be the one who reminds everyone of how tough life is. Instead be the person that inspires others to believe that life is good today and will be better tomorrow. I truly believe that every reader who reflects objectively on their own character in this regard can improve their own personal happiness and relationships in some manner by working to be more positive in all aspects of their life.

Don't Be Self-Centered

Me-ism is the grand slayer of countless billions of relationships. Being self-centered is usually viewed as one of the most unappealing personality traits in a potential friend, lover, or business partner. Self-centered people typically put themselves first, only care about their own wants, and often are incapable of seeing another person's perspective and needs. For any type of relationship to endure the test of time, it must be mutually satisfying and beneficial. Successful relationships are always based on an even balance of give and take. It does not make a difference whether it is a friendship, love, or business; everyone involved must have something of value to bring to the table so to speak. Our society seems to be headed in the wrong direction in regards to this ugly trait, so take an objective look at yourself. If you focus on self-improvement in this area, you'll definitely see improvement in all of your relationships and even in your business dealings.

Don't Be a Gossip

Gossiping is always a betrayal of trust and inevitably destructive to relations. True friends never gossip. Commenting in a positive manner about someone is one thing, but revealing too much personal information or sensationalized facts about someone will always result in feelings being hurt. Even if your indiscretion is never discovered, others will lose respect for you. They will assume you will gossip about them too and limit their relationships with you. So preserve your integrity and walk away when others gossip. True friends overlook faults, guard secrets, and protect other people's privacy. Also keep in mind that gossiping tends to be a vicious cycle and that the other gossips will probably tell what you say back to that person. When you gossip about someone then they will talk even more negatively about you, ultimately motivating you to talk more aggressively about them. Since others may prejudge you based on such misinformation, it is best to avoid gossip and its vicious cycles altogether.

Avoid Enemies

I don't mean avoid enemies as in stay out of their way, I mean don't have enemies. Although there will always be a few who view you as their enemy, you should have no enemies. You should work hard on constructive relationships that can produce positive and tangible results. You should completely avoid expending valuable time and energy on nonproductive relationships by not allowing others to lure you into a never ending feud that no one can win. Don't waste your time on such worthless relationships, as this is another one of those vicious cycles that accomplishes nothing. Never hate – just ignore these would be enemies. The more you concentrate your time on problematic people the more they focus on you. Put your time and energy to better use. Be the better person, and turn the other cheek. You will gain the respect of your peers and others who are aware of your situation when you leave pride and pettiness behind while ignoring these types of insecure personalities.

Avoid the Last Straw

Everyone is familiar with the expression the straw that broke the camel's back. You must keep in mind that each negative action of yours adds weight to the burden which is carried by another in your relations. If you are oblivious to others concerns then eventually their back is broken and the relationship ends. On the other hand each unselfish act of yours lightens the load so to speak. Thus you should always strive to find ways of pleasing others. It should be your daily goal to create more positive memories and feelings than negative ones in all your relationships. You need to keep track of your own actions, but not theirs. If a harsh word spoken or some negative action by you leaves your conscience feeling guilty, surely it will add weight to the pile. Therefore when you make mistakes you need to own them, and apologize quickly. A willing apology demonstrates your genuine concern and hopefully takes back the last straw you inadvertently tossed on the pile.

Don't Be a Control Freak

Be a leader, if that is what your character and personality dictate to you. There is always someone who is willing to follow. It is OK to lead, to be in control in this manner; however, it is never a good thing to dominate someone else so completely that they lose their own individuality. Total control and domination will inevitably lead to their dissatisfaction, resentment, and eventually to rebellion. If you have a tendency to be controlling you should choose your battles carefully. Take control in areas of priority and compromise on lesser issues. Remember a good relationship is based on the 50/50 principle. If you are the dominate personality in a relationship then you may be able to control 55/45 or 60/40 of life's situations without destroying your relationship, but you must never forget that total domination and control is not an viable option. Control freaks tend to always want to increase their level of control inch by inch, ultimately destroying all of their relationships; so let the reader beware.

Reflection and Analysis

In good business models, success is most often created by good planning and hard work followed by analysis of the results. Relationships should be built and maintained using this same formula for success. Unfortunately most relationships develop, thrive, and/or die more by chance than by proper planning and strategy. I strongly recommend that you make a daily effort to reflect and analyze on all of the important relationships in your life. Find five or ten minutes a day that you can devote to this important task. It can be on the drive to and from work, in the shower, or on the treadmill at the gym. On my drive to work each day I meditate on my business goals and business relationships. I try to develop a planned goal for that day and decide who I might want to lunch with that day. On the way home, I focus on my personal goals and relationships. If you can get in the habit of doing this daily, you will see a dramatic improvement in all your relationships.

Chapter Two: 12 Basic Ways To Have A Successful Marriage

Love Fearlessly

Express your love and feelings fearlessly. You must allow yourself to love and to be loved. Never hide your feelings from the person you love. Never let walls stand or come between yourself and your spouse. Love often makes us feel weak and out of control, so it is in our nature to hold back or guard a piece of heart even from our closest loved ones. It takes a strong person to surrender fearlessly to this intoxicating feeling, to share ourselves completely. Tell your mate everyday how important they are to you. Show them daily the appreciation they deserve for the things they do for you. Let them know they are loved unconditionally, not only with your words, but also by your actions. Love knows no fear, love has no boundaries, love believes anything is possible, and love never fails. If you can truly love someone in this manner then it is easy for them to love you back in return.

Be Faithful

Monogamy gets a bad rap nowadays as many say it's unnatural, impossible, outdated, and confining. Yet in reality there are many benefits in being faithful to just one person. Monogamy will promote emotional health in your relationships as trust, loyalty, commitment, devotion, and respect are all heightened in monogamous relationships. Monogamy also promotes physical and financial health in your relationship. Your physical health is protected from sexually transmitted diseases as well as from jealous friends, lovers, husbands, and wives. Your financial health is enhanced by being able to focus all your energy and money into one long term endeavor. True love is an unselfish act, as is monogamy. If you truly desire a lasting relationship you should seek to find a monogamous partner, as a non-monogamous partner is much more likely to move on when they find the bigger better deal that pleasures their selfish desires more than you do.

Be Compatible

No two people are perfectly fit to each other but a reasonable level of compatibility is extremely important. So before you jump in, take an objective look at your situation and see how you rate as a couple in these 10 critical areas:

Personality

Lifestyle

Education

Communication and Conversation

Friends

Family

Health and Nutrition

Finances and Spending Habits

Intimacy and Sexuality

Religion and Spirituality

Be Devoted

Encarta Dictionary defines being devoted as "feeling or showing great love, commitment, or loyalty to somebody or something, especially over a long period of time". To be successfully happy you must be 100 percent devoted to both your mate and your relationship. You must be stubbornly committed not to throw in the towel the first time that conflict arrives. The fact you are reading this book shows commitment to both your partner and relationship. Striving for self-improvement is also an act of your devotion. To fulfill the second half of this definition you must remain devoted "over a long period of time". So do not be a quitter. When times are tough it is essential that you communicate that your devotion is still strong. I like to ask my wife during or after an argument, "You know it is going to take a lot more than this to make me stop loving you, right?" Seems this question always helps to diffuse tensions and put lesser things back into their proper perspective.

Don't Be Judgmental

While I understand it is easy for people to form opinions based on the actions of others, it is extremely important in your personal relationship not to be excessively judgmental of your loved one. Focusing on every little negative aspect of your mate will usually only generate other negative feelings, which over a long period of time will inevitably deteriorate your love and respect for them. You must always think positive and be positive in all aspects of your relationship. You must accept even your mate's faults. You must be extremely careful not to automatically attribute bad motives to your loved one's actions. If they do something that is disturbing to you then it is best to confront them honestly and respectfully, instead of instantly judging them and letting negative feelings develop. It is much better to ask them why they behaved or acted a certain way. Maybe they can help you understand why they chose to act the way they did.

No Emotional Baggage

If you have been hurt in the past, whether in your upbringing or a previous relationship, you must learn to leave all that emotional baggage behind. Give your heart completely and unconditionally to your new love. Each relationship should have a completely fresh and trusting beginning – a clean slate so to speak. Never attribute bad motives to your new partner's actions. You must forget your old wounds and not be preoccupied by subconscious fears and trust issues from your past. Through deliberate reflection and self-examination you must become consciously aware of any baggage that potentially can destroy your new relationship. If you don't understand your own emotional baggage, your partner's baggage, and the triggers that so often bring these pains to the surface then you are at the mercy of these subconscious feelings. Do not let old emotional baggage from previous situations ruin your current relationship. Start fresh and be mentally aware to leave the past where it belongs.

Don't Be a Perfectionist

The perfectionist tends to seek perfection in every aspect of their life, including their relationships. Perfectionists often have many issues that develop in their personal lives because of these unattainable goals. By setting impossibly high standards, the perfectionist cannot help but find disappointment and flaws in every relationship. Their obsessive behavior often creates unsustainable levels of negative energy in their relationships. Not being satisfied with their own accomplishments most perfectionists tend to dismiss praise, advice, and compliments from their partner. This naturally can be quite frustrating to their loved one. Their relationships also suffer when the mate is unable to sustain the level of positive feedback that the perfectionist requires. Thus to succeed the perfectionist must learn to accept flaws in themselves and others, and their spouses need to offer strong re-assurance that the perfectionist is loved, even if they are not perfect.

Be a Little Unpredictable

Routine can kill any type of relationship, but this is especially true in long-term personal relations. Being predictable can make your life boring and unfulfilled. Men especially tend to be content with routines, so we must make a conscious effort not to get trapped in a rut that leads us away from the women we love. On the other hand, variety and excitement can make life rich and rewarding. Be imaginative; keep your mate always guessing what you might do next. A gift for no reason, unexpected phone calls, dance impulsively, leave a love note someplace unusual like the dishwasher or the underwear drawer, tell someone you love them at a different time of the day than usual, and changing sexual patterns are just a few possible suggestions. Ask your loved one, "East or west?", and then take them for an unexpected drive wherever they chose. You might be surprised what you find. Be creative, be impulsive, but most importantly try to always be a little unpredictable.

Leave Stress at Work

Had a bad day at work? Do you feel uptight and stressed out every day after work? That's OK and normal, but it is imperative for your physical health and the emotional health of your relationship that you relieve stress as quickly as possible at the end of each day. It is extremely important that you be consciously aware to leave all of your negative energy and feelings behind you before arriving home. You must never take your stress home with you, and you definitely must not take it out on your family and loved ones. They don't deserve that and you know it. There is nothing that relieves work related stress better than a hard work out. A relaxing shower, a brisk walk, a run in the park, or a daily stop at the gym can also be a refreshing end to a hard day's activities. A short stop somewhere for a few minutes of reading and meditation or listening to relaxing music on the drive home are other proven techniques that can help you to arrive home with a fresh and peaceful attitude.

The Power of Laughter

Laughter has been studied for its medicinal qualities. It is now known that laughter relaxes tense muscles, reduces stress levels, sends more oxygen into your system quicker, and lowers your blood pressure while improving heart functioning. A good laugh even has the power to help heal our bodies and overcome chronic pain. The expression laughter is the best medicine can definitely be applied directly to your relationships. Like smiles, laughter has the ability to reinvigorate a lackluster relationship. Laughter, humor, and playfulness are potent communication utilities that can create a powerful sense of intimacy and bonding in your relationships. Laughter lightens your burdens, inspires hopes, and even can diffuse conflict. Best of all, this precious medicine is completely free and easy to use. I recommend a high dosage of this intoxicating medicine be taken at least four or five times a day. Humor and shared laughter are essential elements in all strong, healthy relationships.

Don't Avoid Confrontation

I know at first thought this sounds backwards, but confrontation can be a good thing for many reasons when approached with respect and honesty. Many times your spouse may not even realize how much their actions are upsetting you if you don't tell them. Conflict resolution can also help prevent resentment from starting or building to intolerable levels. You should never feel bad or wrong about identifying a conflict or initiating a confrontation to resolve it. Confrontations are a natural component of all healthy relationships and can be done in constructive manner, especially if you are mentally prepared to avoid anger and emotional outbursts. The tone and timing of your approach is most critical to your success. Never confront your mate when angry. Always have the correct wording planned ahead and be prepared for a potential outburst from them. Keep your words soft and your ears open. Be willing to listen and understand their viewpoint too.

Avoid Addicts & Addiction

Trust my experience on this – you never willingly want to compete with an addiction. An addiction is generally understood to be an unhealthy craving for anything to such an extent that it creates problems for the individual, their lives, their work, and their families. Addictions tend to expose weaknesses in character that usually over time will destroy relationships. If you see any symptoms of addiction in your potential spouse it is best to run. If you are an addict then you must deal with your own addiction before starting any new relationships. It really makes no difference whether someone is addicted to drugs, alcohol, food, gambling, or even sex. An addict's physical and/or psychological dependencies will inevitably lead to compulsive and destructive behaviors. More often than not, an addict will choose their addiction over everything else, including their mate. Avoid addicts and addiction, if you want your relationship to succeed.

Chapter Three: 50 Ways To Be A Better Mate

Communicate Your Feelings

Communication is essential to all successful relationships. It is important that you are able to share all of your feelings with your partner. You must communicate your love and commitment if you want your love to endure. It does not matter how much you love someone, if they don't know or understand it. You must also share your dislikes and concerns too so that resentment, frustration, and anger doesn't develop over time. The more you share with your mate the more they can understand and support you. Thus you should never hide anything as feelings are not necessarily right or wrong. Share your weaknesses and your strengths, your fears and your hopes, and your pain as well as your joy. It is best to share any developing feelings as soon as you begin to recognize that they exist. By exposing in advance your innermost feelings, your partner will have more empathy and understanding of you when anger, stress, and/or conflict develop later.

Listen to Criticism

I know, criticism hurts, especially when it comes from someone we love. However, it is important to remember that criticism is a form of communication. In a healthy relationship there should be enough love and trust to be able to give and receive productive criticism to one another. You and your mate should always have a strong commitment to communicate openly with integrity and respect. Although no one is fond of receiving criticism, it can actually be very constructive when you are able to learn from it. People who criticize you to your face normally have a vested interest, so it is best for you to listen objectively to what they have to say before responding. Through self-analysis, mutual problem solving, and negotiation criticisms that are founded on truth can lead to improvement in your character and relationships. Your acceptance and positive response to justifiable criticism will strengthen the bonds between you and your loved one.

Be Self-Sufficient

Self-sufficiency is defined as being able to provide for oneself without the help of others; being able to live independently of others. Unfortunately many people, especially younger people, often leave the security of their parent's home and immediately seek this same security in the arms of another. They never learn to be self-sufficient first. They never master being happy alone. They frequently find themselves, and their partner, unprepared to take care of each other or sometimes even their own family. They often enter a relationship with the unconscious expectation that the other person will care for them in whatever ways they had been provided for in the past by their parents or others. Unfortunately often their life partner is expecting the same care from them. Thus I strongly recommend you learn self-sufficiency first. Learning to thrive in a relationship will be much easier to master if you are already a self-sufficient individual.

Set Clear Boundaries

Relationships work harmoniously when everyone knows what to expect and what is expected of them. Many of the dos and don'ts in this book are basic boundaries that I am recommending. Since boundaries vary by person and between situations you must learn to set boundaries for yourself. Whenever possible, it is best to clearly set boundaries early in a relationship before conflict arises or an unspoken boundary is crossed. When establishing boundaries it is best to speak in the "I" and not with the word "you", so you appear non-accusing. Remain calm, kind, and confident. Remember, the tone of your voice most often decides whether a conflict is resolved peacefully or escalates. People with low self-esteem often have problems setting boundaries as they are dependent on the approval of others. If this you, you must first learn to love and respect yourself before you will have the strength and courage to set boundaries in a successful relationship with someone else.

Don't Be Materialistic

"Materialism is toxic for happiness," says University of Illinois psychologist Ed Diener. Many studies into the consequences of pursuing a materialistic lifestyle find that it is negatively related to life satisfaction and overall happiness in personal relationships. Though we all need material possessions to survive and enjoy life, studies show that being too materialistic is damaging to one's physical and mental health as well as to relationships. People who seriously pursue materialistic values tend to treat others as objects. They ultimately encounter problems developing long lasting relationships, as they often face conflict and feelings of alienation in their personal lives. Materialistic people tend to work too much, stress too often, and ignore the people that they love. They invariably feel pressured and controlled by life events. Instead of feeling free and autonomous, they often feel empty and enslaved. So be happy, not materialistic.

Don't Be Megalomaniac

Though megalomania is defined by the Merriam-Webster online dictionary as "a delusional mental disorder that is marked by feelings of personal omnipotence and grandeur", more recent research shows megalomania is not always a mental disorder. It really depends on a matter of degree, but it is important to understand that superiority complexes and relationships are geometrically opposed to one another. It is usually impossible for the megalomaniac to give their life partner the respect they deserve. In a relationship it should be your goal to draw closer to your partner, while megalomaniacs tend to separate themselves from others by treating other people as inferior and displaying many narcissistic qualities that cause resentment. Confidence or the proper use of power in a relationship is one thing, even arrogance or large egos can be tolerated by some individuals; but megalomaniacs are rarely successful in any of their relationships as their behavior is unacceptably off balanced in everyone's perspective but their own.

Be Passionate About Life

Never settle with ordinary, be extraordinary. Take life on head first. Passionate people often believe success is inevitable. If you believe - then you will succeed, not only in what you accomplish, but also in inspiring hope and admiration in others. Being passionate about life has the ability to change your perception of everything you will encounter in life. It can bring satisfaction and happiness to even mundane areas of life like work. People who are passionate about anything usually have the ability to look past the difficulties and challenges of life, as they can only see a future filled with dreams that will soon come true. Passion will motivate you and give you a superior level of confidence. True passion for life will set you free and make you feel uninhibited, releasing you from unnecessary worries and stress. Passion is a very contagious and magnetic quality. It draws others to you and makes you feel appreciated by them. Always let your life partner see your passion for life as well as your passion for your relationship with them.

Don't Be a Complainer

Chronic complaining is damaging to all relationships, as healthy relations are built on happiness and other positive feelings, not negativity and dissatisfaction. Complaining is a destructive habit that is highly contagious and can start a vicious cycle in your relationship, especially if the complaints are aimed directly at your loved one or their actions. Empathy is the attention that complainers are often seeking, so if you see yourself as a chronic complainer then you need to examine yourself and your subconscious motivations. If your life partner is the complainer, confrontation in a constructive way is usually required to end this damaging and negative behavior. You must set clear boundaries and be brutally honest with the complainer. When a chronic complainer starts complaining, offer a little empathy and one solution to whatever is upsetting them. If the complaining continues then tell the person directly you would rather discuss something more positive and up building.

Be Proactive, Not Reactive

Don't hesitate to deal with issues when they are small and manageable. You can only prevent major issues from developing in your relationship if you can recognize the potential problem in advance. Honest, objective analysis is required for you to develop the insight and ability to be proactive. Many times the issue can be more in your own mind and attitude than in reality. At times like this you must have the humility to see that the issue is in your own perspective. Issues like these can be resolved by being more positive in your thinking and more grateful of your mate's overall qualities. In other cases, if something your partner is saying or doing begins to be a source of irritation then don't wait until frustration and resentment have grown to the point of anger and conflict. Confrontation, when approached with good planning and forethought, is always better than conflict after you reached your boiling point. Being proactive, to a large extent, depends on your ability of self-awareness.

Avoid Being Revengeful

There is no room for revenge in any successful relationship. Revenge can only undermine the love, respect, and trust that should exist between you and your partner. By its nature revenge divides couples and pits them against each other. It really makes no difference if you have been offended in a major or minor way. Tit for tat is definitely a losing game for couples. All acts of revenge will inevitably cause a relationship to begin spiraling into pain and negativity. Any act of revenge will only aggravate existing problems in your relationship or possibly inspire your partner to try and outdo you. Any immediate sense of vindication that you might gain from an act of revenge will likely be replaced with remorse when your conscience kicks in gear. Additional anger and conflict will most likely result too, causing further strife and misery in your relations. So don't seek revenge, seek unity through proper communication and mutual understanding.

Avoid Extreme Jealousy

If you display no jealousy, your mate will consider you cold, heartless, or without love and genuine affection for them. If you are too jealous then you will be labeled as possessive, controlling, and unreasonable. So jealousy is like walking the high wire at the circus, you must not lean too far either way if you hope for success. When you feel jealous it is best to show it to your partner, but you must do so in a manner that is productive. Showing a reasonable amount of jealousy and concern will make your partner feel loved and appreciated. Discussing your feelings also helps to set mutually acceptable boundaries in your relationship. If something your partner is doing is disturbing you it is better to discuss it immediately. A good way to approach such a conversation is with humor. When I begin to feel jealous I like to ask my wife if I need to call my friends Bruno and Guido to explain to the culprit's face whatever emotions I am feeling.

Never Panic or Overreact

Panic is contagious. If you tend to respond instinctively in negative manners then you must master your own reactions before you can smoothly guide your relationship around potential problems. Panic is a sign of weakness, so be strong for your relationship and loved one. The minute you begin to feel a surge of negative emotions then take a deep breath. Think clearly before speaking. A moment of silence can often tell your partner as much as an outburst of anger. Don't be afraid to even call a timeout. Telling your partner in firm but loving voice that you need to discuss this in a few minutes after you have composed yourself can be a good approach to resolving a serious issue that has your blood boiling. They will know how much the issue has disturbed you, but your attempt to remain in control will earn their respect and cooperation in resolving the conflict. So remember to never panic, to never overreact. Always stay calm, think first, and respond only when you are in complete control.

Be Balanced

To be a well-rounded person and an attractive mate, it is necessary to have balance in all areas of life. Achieving balance most often means cutting back on extremes. You need to find balance between your life and work, your friends and your relationship, your spending and your savings, and your serious times and your good times. In these areas almost anything can be permissible, if it is only done on rare occasions. It is extremely important in successful relationships that there is some balance in the sharing of power. Naturally many conflicts in relationships are really about control and power, so this is one area where balance is truly needed. Another area where balance is needed is in how you relate to your mate. It is easy to suffocate your loved one by being a clinging vine. It is easy to drive them way by being too distant. Space is necessary in all relationships, but you must never confuse space with distance. Be balanced in all things.

Learn From Mistakes

By identifying the causes of your previously failed relationships, you can often put yourself in a better position to improve your current or next relationship. In past relationships you should always look primarily at yourself, the choices made by you, your actions, and also your reactions. Focus your analysis on things in your control. Look at things you can possibly change, prevent, or improve upon now. Look for patterns, especially in your the choice of partners and the mistakes that led past relationships to fail. If you are in a current relationship, you can also learn from any mistakes you might encounter here too. By examining any mistakes, issues, or problems you might be encountering with your current partner you will be able to learn their weaknesses and what might trigger future problems. If you are observant and open-minded you should also be able to see areas where you can find avenues to be helpful and supportive of them in the future.

Have Self-Control/Self Discipline

Self-control has been defined as the faculty of conscious and deliberate action. It is the power we have to choose our own response and actions. Self-control is strongly associated with what we label success, and this is particularly true in relationships. In relationships self-discipline and control take many forms. Sometimes your loved one will enrage you accidentally. Sometimes your partner may try to test or provoke you deliberately. Either way it is necessary to control your own action or words when you feel in an aggressive mood. Restraint can be very difficult to learn, so mental preparation is mandatory in all cases. If you are prepared for most probabilities, then you should be able to respond constructively in these situations instead of negatively. A positive response to negative stimuli is not easy, but learning and acting positive in all situations will gain your life partner's love, respect, and cooperation.

Be Agreeable

A very big secret to stress free relationships is learning to master the skill of being agreeable. Try not to outright judge your partner. Try not to make everything about right and wrong, especially over small and petty things. Don't believe if one person is right then the other person must be wrong. This way of thinking disagreeably inevitably causes stress and frustration in your relationship that will lead to tension and arguments. Small differences should just be accepted unconditionally. When something is important enough to express outright disagreement, you can still be agreeable by respecting their opinion as much as possible. Never say, "That's wrong!" Instead you should say, "Well I can understand that point of viewpoint, but I think …" Being agreeable means be willing to listen, even if they have opposing views and being tactful enough to disagree in an agreeable manner. You should also remember that a person who is capable of agreeing to disagree is an agreeable partner.

Stay Focused

You must stay focused in several ways. First don't just let your relationship steer itself, you must always be in conscious control and guide it. A second key to all successful relationships is to stay focused on being harmonious and positive. When a relationship starts, everything is normally easy as both persons are focusing on the good, instead of the differences. Unfortunately as relationships progress, the focus usually changes from the positive aspects to the negatives. If you lose focus on the good, then your relationship will ultimately head downhill. When the negatives become more obvious you must just focus on conflict resolution. And finally, you must focus primarily on yourself. Pay attention carefully to what you are putting put into the relationship on a day to day basis. When you focus on the relationship, cooperation, and contributing positive energy to the relationship then your loved one will follow along instinctively. Clear focus will always net positive results.

Ignore Small Faults

We all have faults, and most of us are very sensitive about our weaknesses and deficiencies. Attacking someone's insecurities is very destructive to your relationship with them, as it will builds up walls between you and them. Successful relationships are built on trust and understanding, so people tend to open up to those who are capable of accepting them unconditionally. Thus you must choose your battles carefully, confront major issues only while overlooking small faults. Remember too that everyone is on their own path, learning what they need to learn as they pass through life day to day. So what you may view as a fault or imperfection they may or may not have discovered as an issue yet. Especially when it comes to quirks, nervous habits, social interaction, and other things such as these there may be no right or wrong. Maybe the fault in is your perception of the world and not in the reality of the moment.

Be Respectful

When you offer respect to someone, it is almost always equally returned. Love and respect are closely intertwined. Respect always starts with you; if you don't have respect for yourself then it is very difficult to have respect for others. If you lack self-respect, it is easy to belittle or degrade others in an effort to raise yourself up. Also you cannot ask for respect if you don't give it to your partner. Respect means controlling your feelings and talking about them, not venting your insecurities onto your loved one. Respect means accepting your partner and their faults unconditionally. Respect also means honoring predetermined boundaries. Your respect will make your mate feel secure and comfortable whenever you are around. Respect also involves listening to your partner and valuing their thoughts, ideas and opinions – even in situations where there may be criticism or confrontation that is offered to you in good faith.

Be Thankful

Saying thank you is a very simple thing to do. It only takes a second, but it can warm someone's heart for much longer. I truly believe that we should always say thank you as this small act of appreciation encourages more generosity, and generosity is usually contagious in a successful relationships. It has been said that there is more happiness in giving than receiving, and this is especially true when the giving is appreciated and valued by the small act of saying thank you. In all types of relationships when someone pleases us then we feel challenged to please them too. This is true whether the relationship is based on friendship, love, or business. All successful relationships are positive in nature and full of good vibes. Every little word we speak to others invokes a reaction whether it is negative or positive. Saying thank you invokes a positive reaction every time. Saying thank you is good for business and it is good for your love life too.

Be Polite

Seems like being polite would be common sense, but unfortunately the reality is most people relax their politeness once a relationship reaches the intimacy stage. This is not necessarily a bad thing so long as both parties are in mutual agreement. Unfortunately relaxing our level of politeness too much may be interpreted as a decrease in caring and respect by our friends and partners in life. Many times this can increase their sense of displeasure and lead the relationship away from intimacy. Often such negatives feelings start slowly and build into larger issues over time. It can be very difficult to spot the subtle effects of what is happening in the subconscious mind of someone. Thus I strongly recommend that to maintain a healthy relationship it is best to never relax your level of politeness with the person you love. Being polite is a simple demonstration of love and respect. If you maintain politeness at home, it will then come natural to you in all your other relationships in life too.

Be a Confidence Builder

You should always be supportive of your partner. It is extremely important that you make them feel they can conquer the world. It should always be your goal to help them to become a better and stronger person. It is imperative to remember that your happiness is tied directly to their happiness. If your partner feels unfulfilled, inadequate, or insecure then these negative types of feelings will inevitably carry over into other aspects of your relationship. You should always act like you are the president of their personal fan club. Praise them and their efforts even if they don't always accomplish what they start. Help them to reach their personal goals by being a good coach and supportive partner. Compliment their good qualities while overlooking their faults; and most importantly, you must always speak highly of your mate in front of friends, family, and others. This will help them to have confidence in themselves and in your relationship with them.

Manage Your Time Wisely

Manage your time like it is money, spend it carefully. Make sure that your priorities are correct when it comes to time management and your relationship. Sit down and write a schedule, you may be shocked to find out how much wasted time exists in your week. It is easy to have good intentions but then get swept away by life's swift currents. Being committed to your mate means spending time with them. If you ignore them too much they may find someone else who will devote time to them. Make sure that the time you can spend with them is quality time. Look carefully and you can remove distractions from the time you spend with your mate. Turn off your cell phone whenever possible. Read your newspaper on your breaks at work or listen to the news on the drive home instead of at home. Use your lunch time and breaks to accomplish simple tasks, like paying bills or balancing your checkbook; this will free up more personal quality time at home.

Be Generous

When it comes to relationships, generosity is not always about money. It should be about much more than that. Besides sharing money, there are at least five more significant ways of being generous in your relationships. First and foremost, you must be generous with your time. Time is a valuable commodity. Making time for your loved one reinforces in their mind that your love is genuine and they are your priority. Second, be generous with words. Kind words and good conversation will strengthen the bonds that exist between you. Third, be generous with acts of kindness. This is self-explanatory but don't forget to think of them every time you think of yourself. Fourth, be generous with your thanks. Remember, appreciation is a form of love. And last but not least, be generous with physical contact. Hold their hand, hug, and kiss your mate more they need and expect. Remember to think of your life partner's sexual needs, preferences, and pleasure as much as you do your own.

Be Thrifty With Money

Being thrifty can make you and your partner's dreams come true. The less money you waste the more money you will have to spend on material items that can improve your life. Being thrifty can also be practical and healthy in another way. When it comes to day to day expenses, it is very easy to allow your expenses to control your life and inadvertently this can directly affect your level of stress and happiness. Stress has a direct effect on your physical health as well as the health of your relationship. The more stress you have in your life the more likely you will interact poorly with the people you love most. Also the more time you spend meeting your financial obligations the less opportunity you will have to enjoy quality time with your loved ones. As money issues are one of the most common factors cited in divorces, being thrifty can definitely be advantageous and thus help to make your relationship strong and stable.

Exercise

Naturally everyone wants a partner who is physically fit and appealing to others. However exercise is not only good for your body and your sex appeal, it also is good for your mood and self-esteem too. Exercise will make you pleasing to yourself as well as put you in a relaxed state of mind. People tend to do better in relationships when they feel positive about themselves and have lots of self-respect. Exercise is also proven to be a good stress relieving activity. By removing stress through physical activity you indirectly help your relationship by leaving unnecessary stress outside of the home. Another benefit of exercise is that it improves your sex drive. It helps you to have the strength and stamina you need to please your mate better when sexual activities actually begin. Exercising with your partner will also improve their sex drive, as physical closeness and touching is always the first step towards inspiring sex in the bedroom.

Be a Good Dresser

The fact is your life partner does notice what you look like and how you present yourself, no matter how much they strive to be open-minded. Naturally we put our best foot forward when relationships first start, so we often dress to impress. Later we tend to dress down as we feel more comfortable with each other. At home and in day to day activities it should be OK to be yourself so to speak, even if you are a little farther out there than most. However, there are certain times when you need to show consideration for your loved ones by wearing the appropriate clothes for certain events and occasions. If in doubt don't hesitate to ask for their opinion, which they may hesitate to give if you don't. If they do ask," Are you really going to wear that?" then remember the correct and considerate answer should always be, "Of course not, dear. I was just checking to see if it still fits. What do you think I should wear?"

Don't Be a Neat Freak or Slob

Be neat when you can be neat, yet be reasonable about your expectations. It only takes a second to put something away once you are done using it, so don't let it become a source of irritation. In relationships we must share space as well as love. Always seek compromise, especially when you and your mate may have different standards for maintaining different areas you share. Try to compromise on different standards for different rooms, cars, etc. If you are the neat freak you should assume responsibility for your own expectations. Look objectively at your own standards. If your expectations are higher than most people's then don't expect your partner to maintain your standards. Do it yourself and allow your partner to maintain his private areas at more reasonable standards. If you are the slob personality you must compromise by maintaining a higher standard in spaces that are shared or more public like the living room or bathroom.

Share in the Chores

It is amazing how a small thing like chores can have huge effects on your relationship. Failing to share in the chores most often will lead to resentment and inevitably conflict. Sometimes its effects are subtle while other times they are immediately obvious. Over time the person doing the chores will eventually feel they are putting more into the relationship than the other, and these negative feelings will usually show themselves in destructive ways in the relationship. It is a simple act of consideration to share in the chores. It shows your commitment to the family unit. It shows your loved one you are unselfishly committed to the relationship, even in the routine ways of life. Research shows that couples who share in the chores tend to have better sex lives than couples who don't. Research also shows that families who share in chores together also have children who are better behaved and better adjusted socially in school and in life.

Never Embarrass Your Loved One

Embarrassing anyone undermines the pillars of trust and respect that are important to that relationship. There are many ways we can inadvertently humiliate our loved one. Sharing personal details is a definite no no. Discussing their faults or past mistakes with others is an act of betrayal that is usually considered traitorous. Naturally you don't want to have arguments in front of friends and family. When there are issues, it is important that you don't try to demonstrate who wears the pants in your house. Flexing your muscles in this manner will only cause frustration and resentment. Disputes should be handled as discreetly and privately as possible. And of course we don't want to laugh at their expense in front of others. A good story may make your friends laugh, but the price you may pay when you are alone later may be higher than you expect. Remember your discretion in such matters demonstrates your love and respect for your mate.

Avoid Too Much TV

Actually it is my personal belief that whenever two people are together the TV should be completely banished. I recommend that each person watch their own TV in their own private time. When couples are together they should focus on each other. It is not that there is anything fundamentally wrong with enjoying an occasional show together, but unfortunately the reality is that TV is designed to entertain and distract viewers. Whenever the TV gets turned on, inadvertently your relationship gets turned off. To be a good partner you should have some household rules set regarding TV. If you cannot or don't want to banish it completely, I strongly recommend you set a predetermined limit of TV time and you constantly monitor the TV's effects on your relationships. There is much research showing TV and computer use being directly tied to weak relationships. There is also much research showing less TV improves your sex life.

Choose Friends Wisely

New relationships often force us to re-prioritize our time and our existing friendships too. When unexpected conflict develops between your partner, who normally is considered your best friend, and your other friend(s) you must try to look objectively at everyone and determine who is being a good friend in this case. Here are five things to consider in resolving a situation of conflict between friends: (1) A true friend will be accepting of other friends in general. (2) A friend does not compete with or sabotage relationships and looks out for the best interests of others. (3) A friend may on occasion give advice that is difficult to hear. (4) A friend won't ignore, disrespect, or embarrass their friend in front of other people or friends. (5) A friend will seek compromise when conflict arises. So who is to blame? You? Yes, I did ask if it was you, so re-read the questions and consider yourself first. Or is it your partner or the other friend(s) that is to blame?

Have a Sense of Humor

A good sense of humor is an attractive quality. It will help you to connect with people in all forms of relationships – personal, family, and business. Humor and inside jokes are very healthy for relationships as it bonds people together. In fact laughter is a good indicator of happiness in general and can be used to measure the health of a relationship. It indicates that two people are relaxed and at ease with each other. If you think you lack a good sense of humor don't fret or give up. Humor is something that is learned, not inherited. You can improve your sense of humor by carefully observing others. Watch and learn before practicing with close friends and family. Soon you can be the "life of the party" yourself. A good sense of humor can also relieve stress and diffuse tense moments in a relationship, especially if you use self-deprecating humor to neutralize conflicts. However, don't forget, humor should never be used to belittle the people you love.

Get a Good Night's Sleep

Sleep deprivation is very damaging to your health and to the health of your relationships. Negativity, irritability, lack of patience, and even an increase in sarcasm have all been shown in various studies to increase when we do not sleep well. There are also research projects that undeniably show a clear association exists between your sleep quality and the quality of your relationships. Your previous night's sleep directly affects the quality of your next day's relationship, and relationship functioning of one day directly affects your subsequent night's sleep. Thus it is extremely important to get a good night's sleep every night to avoid starting a vicious cycle of deteriorating relations. Resolving ongoing disputes quickly will prevent negative thoughts and meditation from interfering with a good night of rest. By resolving conflicts before going to bed you will improve your sleep quality and help to avoid such a vicious cycle from beginning to develop.

The Strength of Smiles

A smile may be what started you on the path to a lifetime friendship with your spouse. A smile can brighten someone's day. A smile can diffuse a tense moment. And a smile can even restore the pillars of a lackluster relationship. Smiles can definitely improve your marriage in many ways. Thus it should be your continual goal to find ways to make your partner smile on a daily basis. The most proven way to invoke a smile is to smile first, so always be positive and happy. When your spouse is stressed, tired, or under some sort of pressure, then that is when you need take control of the situation and make them smile. Hug them, kiss them, and/or tell them you love them. Don't be afraid to be creatively funny at times. Be goofy, make faces, give them those eyes, imitate them, or threaten to tickle them if they don't smile. Do whatever it takes. Remember one of the important keys to a successful relationship is making your mate smile every time you walk in the room.

Read a Book per Year

Self-improvement is a science, and self-motivation is an art. Therefore you need to devote yourself to the study of these very important subjects. These topics if reviewed periodically can stimulate growth in all areas of your life. Reading self-improvement books often leads to new ideas, wisdom, successes, and happiness. Also your mate will likely view your reading habit as a commitment to being a better person and a netter mate. This why I recommend you read a self-improvement book at least once a year. It does not matter what area of self-improvement appeals to you. There is always something positive to be gained; however, as you read these books you should always consider how the author's recommendations will affect your closest relationships. Everything that we do in our lives directly impacts our personal relationships. Thus we should regularly meditate and review how our recent successes and failures are influencing the people we love most in our lives.

Don't Be a Clinging Vine

A clinging vine is a person who tends to behave in a helpless and dependent manner in their relationships, though they often are submissive and faithful mates. People who enter a relationship with a clinging vine personality often like the attention and have a desire to be needed, thus their dependency is at first appealing. Inevitably other negative qualities become more obvious later as clinging vine personalities are usually possessive, jealous, and suffering from a lack of self-love too. Eventually the dependency and needs of a clinging vine will become a burden, even a weight around the neck of their partner. In time most people feel suffocated, trapped, or tired out by the needs of the clinging vine they chose. If you see yourself as a clinging vine, then you must learn to be more self-sufficient and happy alone. You also must learn to allow your loved ones their own freedom, so you don't chase away the people you love most in your life. By finding you own independence you will find more balance and happiness in your relationships.

But Don't Be Overly Independent Either

Overly independent people tend not to build deeper commitment and intimacy in their relationships. Inevitably their mates feel something lacking in the relationship when they realize the overly independent person is excessively cold, distant, and detached. Connecting at a deeper level enables you to share more of your genuine self. This leads to more meaningful and longer-lasting relationships. Revealing your true self to others requires trust and often leaves you vulnerable, yet true intimacy requires this commitment. I like to view proper dependency in a relationship like holding hands. Both people should want to be together. Yet neither partner should carry the other as is the case with a clinging vine personality, and neither should be so independent that they end up walking off alone. Balance and compatibility are essential in finding a happy level of inter-dependency. Figuratively speaking, a well-balanced and happy couple likes to hold hands.

The Effects of Your Scent

Perfume and colognes have always been widely associated with attracting a mate. The majority of women and the vast majority of men prefer someone who is scented to someone who is unscented. When properly used, without overdosing your partner's nose, a lightly scented body is appealing to most people. Even if your mate is part of the minority who prefers an unscented body, your personal hygiene and bathing practices can affect your natural scent. You can influence your partner's desire to be near you, depending on the odor you omit. Our sense of smell is part of the limbic system in the brain which is directly tied to emotions and memory. Our brains when storing information frequently couple emotion and memory together. Your good body scent is often connected to your mate's desire and emotions surrounding sex. Thus your good scent is a powerful tool that you can use in enticing and staying close to your loved one.

Good Personal Hygiene

Proper sanitary practices are important because they affect your overall wellness, self-confidence, self-esteem, and productivity - as well as all your relationships. When you interact with other people anywhere in your day to day life having bad breath, dirty finger nails, stained teeth, smelly feet, dirty clothes, or being unkempt are major turn offs. Any of these bad habits and impressions can limit your personal contact and communication with other people. Bad personal hygiene is just as critical to avoid in a friendship, business negotiation, or job interview as it is in your relationship. A bad impression in this most important area can kill any type of relationship before it even has the chance to mature. This is especially true in the area of your love life. If your potential life partner is hesitant to be close to you, then it is very difficult to build the intimate bonds and connections that will help you through the difficult times your relationship will inevitably encounter.

Never Ridicule

You may justify ridiculing or laughing at your mate as good-natured teasing, but usually that is not how it is understood by them. In their mind, it is usually viewed as an attack. In reality, ridicule is a personal assault on them. Ridicule can even be verbal abuse. It can create insecure feeling and doubts in your partner's mind. It can cause them to harbor anger and resentment long after the incident should have been forgiven and forgotten. Ridicule can even cause a vicious cycle of malicious and vindictive behavior to develop in your relations. Humiliating someone often causes them to strike back at you in different ways, with them feeling their actions are justified because of your previous behavior. Then when you feel victimized by their recent response, you feel justified in responding in another negative manner towards them. One attack leads to another. Before long it is all out warfare and no one even remembers what caused the war in the first place. Thus you should never ridicule. Just love, support, and accept your partner and their little flaws unconditionally.

Be a Good Coach

Coaching is a skill and a mentoring technique that the corporate world teaches its managers nowadays to develop employees rather than impose their will on the employee by giving him lists of dos and don'ts. Coaching seeks to help the employee understand himself and the importance of his interactions with others. By encouraging reflection instead of giving direction, the employee is enabled to be successful. Through empathy and communication, it is the coach's goal to help the employee find the correct answers by themselves. In relationships this technique can also be quite successful. Being overly demanding of your partner seldom results in the permanent change you are seeking. By asking questions and leading your partner to the proper conclusion on their own, they then feel comfortable embracing your suggested changes willingly. Coaching is a very practical method of molding your partner into a better person, the person that both of you are seeking.

Ask – Don't Reprimand

When someone you love inadvertently hurts, upsets, or disappoints you, it is important that you don't allow your emotions to control the moment. Don't accuse them of anything. Don't assume anything. Don't reprimand them. And whatever you do don't ever rant and rave. These typical types of reactions will not accomplish anything good but will only lead to an out of control emotional argument. The best thing to do is ask questions. Simply ask them why they did or said that? Or ask them if they know how much that hurts you? Or ask them how they would feel if the situation was reversed? Accusations, assumptions, reprimands, and ranting and raving will only provoke a negative and defensive response from your partner. On the other hand, a direct but well-formed question asked politely, while showing your hurt, should make them think clearly about their actions. A good question asked properly will show them how what they have said or done affects you and their relationship with you.

Live in the Moment

It is important to be philosophical and find ways to be happy today, right now in this moment. The power of positive thinking can change your whole outlook on life. Don't let insignificant feelings or frustrations destroy your whole day's happiness. Focus on the good, and find ways to laugh at or make fun of the negative things that can destroy the precious moment in you are in right now. Always maintain your smile. Always find ways to laugh, even if you have to fake it sometimes. Never worry or fret for the future, just do what you can today to make it better. Live and learn from your past, but never let your shame or failures control your future. Just focus on being happy and satisfied with what you have today. Find ways to make the people closest to you happy in this moment too. If you take care of their happiness today, they most often will take care of your happiness the next time you are feeling a little down. Life has shown me that good karma always tends to return to its original source.

Never Make Comparisons

Comparisons never work as they divide a couple by putting someone else in between. Even when the comparison is meant as a compliment it is likely to backfire. Though my advice should apply to both sexes, this is especially true when a man compares his lady to another woman. Just the fact that you have noticed another woman will open a can of worms that won't be easy to close, as physical insecurities are a major insecurity to most women. For this reason you should never compare your lady with another, even if it is intended as a compliment. Instead you should make her feel superior by reminding her how special and beautiful she is in your eyes. Another big no is comparing her to your mother, as most women absolutely hate this. Many times there is a natural jealousy and competition between a wife and her mother-in-law. Comparing the two of them will definitely throw gas on the flames of this already existing fire.

Be Courteous

Courtesy takes many forms in our day to day lives and relationships; however, courtesy should go far beyond just being polite and having good manners. Proper courtesy actually involves more than just greeting people with respect, waiting your turn, or not interrupting when others are speaking. In fact, courtesy shows respect for others at all times and makes people feel valued and appreciated. True courtesy requires you to think about how your actions affect others at all times. So in reality courtesy and unselfishness are closely connected. True courtesy should come from deep in your heart and character, and not just be occasional show we put on for others when we are out in public. If you can learn to be wholeheartedly courteous at all times to your business partners, friends, family, and loved ones then you will have mastered a wonderful and truly attractive quality. It will draw people to you in ways that most people cannot ever imagine.

Be Goal Oriented

Achievement does not usually happen accidentally or by pure luck. Don't let your life and/or relationship just happen to you. Create the type of life and relationship you want through action, leadership, and communication. You should set realistic goals for different areas of your life and relationships, and you should make a consistent effort to take small steps toward them on a daily basis. Communication can be improved, intimacy can be enhanced, conflicts can be avoided and resolved, or you can be a better father or husband but not if you just keep hoping it happens naturally. You must constantly think about these important matters, examining and analyzing all your daily interactions with your mate. You must take some type of positive action everyday so that you can reach whatever your lofty goals are eventually. Set short term and long term goals for yourself with your short term goals being the stepping stones that will help you to reach your loftier and more difficult long term goals.

Know Your Body Language

Everyone knows the importance of good communication in a successful relationship, but unfortunately many don't understand that the majority of communication is done non-verbally through body language. Research shows that facial expressions, hand and body gestures, eye contact, posture, how far you stand away, and even the tone of your voice are given much more importance in meaning than the words you speak. Mastering the use of body language will give you a powerful tool that will help you to connect with others, express what you really mean, avoid unnecessary confrontations and conflicts, and build stronger relationships in your life. Learning to understand all the nonverbal signals you are sending will help you to produce the correct body language to make your partner feel loved and appreciated. Learning to smile when spoken to will help you to always keep open the lines of communication with your mate and loved ones.

Have a Set of Principles

If you have not defined yourself with a personal set of principles then you are going through life adrift, aimlessly meandering wherever your current emotions and circumstances allow you to go. It is nearly impossible to define a relationship with someone else if you have not clearly defined yourself first. So I would suggest you take some time to develop a list of principles that will guide you to being the ideal man or woman you want to be. Post them somewhere conspicuous for now to keep them foremost in your mind and grade yourself occasionally. Here are some examples of principles you might include in your own basic set of principles: To be positive in nature, to be up-building in all aspects of life, to be respectful of others, to never harm others, to always be willing to compromise, to be a good friend to others, to be willing to change and grow, to be accepting of others faults, and to always try to be the better person in every situation.

Recipe for Love

Sharing in the cooking can bond a couple together as much as sharing a plate of food. For those who are able, cooking for your partner is an outright demonstration of love. If you are not able to cook, you can still share in this activity by helping with food and table preparations or by helping clean up after a meal. Your willingness to help as much as possible in this daily chore will most often be appreciated and recognized as an act of love on your part. Cooking meals together can definitely strengthen a relationship as couples who cook together inevitably spend more quality time together. Cooking time, like meal times, is a good chance for couples to interact and enjoy each other's company and conversation. Cooking meals together on a regular basis will add stability to your relationship. This time together will also provide you a great opportunity to plan the day's activities in the morning or to catch up on and stay informed on missed events in the evening.

Chapter Four: 40 Ways To Make Your Mate Feel Loved

Date Night

Most marriage counselors and relationship experts strongly recommend that you continue to date your spouse or loved one even after you are married or committed to each other. This is probably the most effective way to keep the romance alive. Scheduling a regular date night is a clear demonstration of commitment to your partner and your relationship with them. It is imperative for your date night to be successful that you view it as an important obligation that cannot be canceled for trivial reasons. Taking a night off regularly is especially needed and even more important for couples with children. Escaping the pressures and routines of daily life to enjoy some good conversation and relaxing time together will refresh your spirits and recharge your batteries. Date nights without the kids will allow you the opportunity for private talk and laughs that will help you maintain the personal bonds that bind you together as a couple. A separate date night for Dad's and kids can also build strong family ties, while giving Mom a needed break.

Pet Names and Nicknames

There is great power and personal connection to be found in nicknames and pet names. Normally pet names don't begin until a certain level of commitment or comfort has been achieved with someone. Thus these expression typically make others them feel special and give them a warm feeling deep down inside, especially the first time someone feels comfortable enough to use one of these terms of endearment. Private pet names often have additional meaning and personal connection as couples share their most intimate and personal feelings, even sometimes their faults. For example, "turtle" could be a loving private nickname for someone dear to you who moves slowly or has a hunched back but probably should not be used in public. Remember to love and respect your partner by not embarrassing them in front of family and friends with exceptionally private nicknames that may be fun and humorous at home but slightly more embarrassing in a public setting.

Love Notes

Everyone expects a love note on Valentine's Day, but unexpected and spontaneous loves notes are the best kind. Love notes can be left any place at any time. For example you can leave one in the pots and pans. Now while doing a mundane task your loved one will be pleasantly surprised to find a note saying, "You are so sexy! I hope tonight we can cook up something together." Don't be surprised when you get home to find dinner ready as well as your partner too. Or you can leave one in her cosmetic case saying, "Forget the makeup. You are beautiful to me." Love notes can even be used as motivational aids. For example, if your mate is on a diet you can leave a note on a can of soda or in the cookie jar saying, "I am watching you because I care." Not only will you tell them you love them, you might even make them skip that soda or cookie. Like anything special don't over use love notes. Be creative, sincere, and have fun keeping them guessing when the next one will come.

Poetry

Poetry is nearly impossible to define; although everyone usually agrees it has a natural quality of being romantic, special, and meaningful. It is usually a personal expression of emotion or experience that is designed to evoke or share an emotional response. The debate of defining poetry has been an ongoing battle for centuries. As a wannabe poet myself, I personally think Wordsworth defined poetry best when he said poetry is "the spontaneous overflow of powerful feelings." And what feeling is more powerful than love? So naturally it is most appropriate for you to share your feelings with the person closest to you in the form of poetry from time to time. You don't have to be a poet to find a poem, a lyric, a saying, a quote, or some other written word that emotionally moves you. Though in reality poetry is found in many forms a good rule of thumb is if it touches your heart or moves your soul then it will probably affect your life partner in the same way when you share it with them.

Flowers

Giving flowers to that special person in your life is one of the most effective ways to display your love and affection to them. The gifting of flowers has a long history dating back into ancient China, Greece, Rome, and Egypt. Gifting particular flowers for particular reasons, as we often do now, dates back to the 1700s when Charles II of Sweden introduced the Persian custom of "the language of flowers" to Europe. Today red roses are well known as the flower of love. Other romantic flower options are carnations, Peruvian lilies, orchids, and tulips. The purple hyacinth is usually given to ask for forgiveness. Orchids are the recommended for formal affairs, such as having the boss or in-laws over for dinner. Carnations are most popular for Mother's Day. Bright, colorful, and cheerful flowers are recommended for any get well occasions, and anniversary flowers vary depending on the year of your anniversary. So share your love by sharing some flowers today.

Learn To Slow Dance

If you can't slow dance or ballroom dance, then it is imperative that you learn today because these forms of dancing are like hugging, except with music and rhythm. In my mind, they are without a doubt the best form of nonsexual touching that you can share with your partner because they communicate your love and desire to be close to your loved one. These styles of dancing generate potent signs of affection that will strengthen your love relationships. They build trust and deepen the intimacy connection between two people while creating powerful and positive memories that will bond you together as a couple forever. Since dancing is a form of non-verbal communication between humans, it can also add a new avenue of personal interaction between you and your mate. This wonderful form of non-verbal communication can be additionally enhanced, if you learn to look your partner deeply in the eyes while holding them in your arms.

Accept and Love Their Family

In-laws bring a unique set of problems to many relationships. In-laws often are over protective in nature, and you may never be good enough for their loved one no matter what you do. Often they are subconsciously jealous of the attention your mate gives you. These negative feelings can cause them to inadvertently or even deliberately act out in ways that can be destructive. By recognizing these human tendencies and accepting them unconditionally, you can undermine their ability to create havoc in your relationship. Your complete acceptance and tolerance of them will prevent problems and earn you the love and respect of your mate. You can prevent most major issues by ignoring petty problems and personality quirks, choosing your battles wisely, never staying too long at in laws, never criticizing a mate in front of their family, and allowing your partner to deal with their own family as much as possible when any issues do arise.

Give Chocolates to Your Loved One

The tradition of giving chocolate to someone you love has roots in the belief that chocolate is a love potion. Throughout history, many cultures have believed chocolate to be a powerful aphrodisiac, including the ancient Aztecs and Mayans. In early Mayan culture, chocolate drinks played a significant role in betrothal and marriage ceremonies. Today we now know that chocolate contains a chemical known as phenylethylamine, the same chemical that is released in your brain when you fall in love. So giving chocolates to someone you love is truly one of the most appropriate gifts of love you can give to someone special. Not only will your gift be accepted readily, as almost everyone loves chocolate, it also is proven to make your partner feel the effects of falling in love again. So remind them of their love for you, by giving them chocolates today.

Turn Off Your Phone

Turning off the phone is a simple technique that shows your loved ones how very important and special they are to you. It is my personal belief that in all but extreme cases you should give priority to the most important people in your life by turning off or ignoring your phone during family meals and family events. I also believe that you should end every day with time devoted to your family, meaning no phone calls after a certain hour. You should be using your phone to stay closer to the important people in your life but unfortunately if you are not careful your phone can undermine and interfere with your personal relationships. Taking calls at inappropriate times can be annoying or even disrespectful. Good phone etiquette is mostly common sense but unfortunately I believe we often treat our families with less respect than we do our friends and employers. By ignoring your phone more often you will show your family they are special to you.

A Serenade

A romantic sunset serenade under her window or a surprise but prearranged serenade at a restaurant can be a special and meaningful way of touching the heart of the woman you cherish and love. Though serenades are most commonly thought of as a courting ritual, this does not always have to be the case, as a serenade is really just a unique public display of affection. A romantic song like *My Woman, My Woman, My Wife* by Marty Robbins is an example of a song that could be used by a husband to serenade his wife. If you are extremely brave and have a reasonable good voice you can serenade her yourself. If you are less brave, or musically handicapped like me, then you can hire a group to help you to serenade your beloved or serenade her in the privacy of your bedroom. Other ideal places to prearrange a serenade might include when strolling or sitting at the beach, picnicking in the park, or possibly while enjoying a surprise getaway weekend at a luxury hotel or resort.

Breakfast in Bed

Breakfast in bed is a great way to express your love and begin a love filled day, especially if you can somehow make it a surprise. Planning and preparing ahead the night before often is helpful in pulling off a surprise breakfast. If you are unable to surprise your partner for whatever reason or you get caught trying you can always make their breakfast extra special by asking them what they prefer or volunteering to be 100 percent at their service. Also to make your loved one's breakfast in bed as special as possible you can always add some finishing touches such as a small gift, freshly cut flowers, their favorite magazine or newspaper, a spa voucher or gift certificate to their favorite store, or even a nice greeting card or love letter. If you are unable to cook up a breakfast in bed for whatever reason you can always take them out to unexpected breakfast date at a great little cafe, preferably somewhere relaxing and tranquil like by the lake or near a park.

A Romantic Surprise

Romantic surprises can make your mate feel special and loved while keeping your relationship fresh and vibrant. It seems to be true that if you can keep the romance alive then everything else will always work out just fine. When relationships are fresh and giving, problems appear as mole hills instead of mountains. There are many ways to surprise your partner. Romantic surprises can be as basic as leaving some flowers or chocolates and a note somewhere to be found later in the day. Anything simple like this can make an ordinary day into a moment special for your loved one. Or it can be as involved and as expensive as a planned weekend getaway at a luxury resort. A romantic dinner at home or at a restaurant, a picnic in front of the fireplace, a bedroom full of candles, or a bed with new silk sheets and rose petals are just a few suggestions. Be imaginative, be creative, or look for help online or from friends and family. Just don't ever let the romance die.

Be Proud of Them

Telling your mate how proud you are of them and their accomplishments will make them feel loved and respected. Research tends to show being proud of your spouse offers different comfort to the different sexes. Men find comfort knowing they are trusted and respected while women tend view such compliments as a sign that they are loved and cherished. You can also let your partner know you are proud of them by boasting to friends and families about their good heart, good talents, the things they do for you, or how lost you would be without them. One of the most overlook ways of being proud of your mate is forgetting to tell them directly that they are a good spouse and parent. As a spouse and parent of your children your mate puts in countless unselfish hours taking care of everyone's needs. An occasional compliment recognizing this can have great meaning to them. All their hard work can be justified by a few kind words from you.

Offer a Toast

Words are powerful. Giving a heartfelt toast is a great way to unite yourself with that special someone in your life, whether the toast is given in a public or private setting. If you are in the habit of giving toasts anyway then you should definitely get in the habit of making sure you always make a reference to your loved somewhere in the toast. A romantic toast is a gift you can give your mate at any time or any place if you keep your mind open to the possibility. It can be given at a formal occasion in front of friends and family, at a restaurant, at a quiet dinner for two, or standing in front of the soda machine with your freshly purchased drinks. Your sincerity and the authenticity of your toast will be greatly enhanced when it is appears most obvious that your toast is an impromptu event. Whenever possible hold their hand, look the person directly in the eyes, and speak as lovingly and confidently as possible while offering a toast to them.

Why Do I Love You?

Don't just tell the one you adore that you love them; you must tell them more than that. If you always tell your special someone that you love them with the same three words, then those words will inevitably lose their significance. It is much better if you tell them what you love about them, what you appreciate about them, how much you need them, and how lost you would be without them. I love how you smile. I love it when you hold me like this. I love you more every day. Examples such as these will make your partner feel loved and appreciated. The frequency of your words is also important. If your expressions of adoration are too frequent or always said at the same time of day or after the same event (example: sex) then your words will become ordinary and less meaningful to your mate. Try to find new times and ways to express your love. You will see the best response when your words come naturally at some unexpected moment.

Look Deep In Their Eyes

It is human nature for us to literally believe others are listening or not depending on their eye contact with us. The inability to make or maintain eye contact is seen as a sign of disinterest or inattentiveness. Thus eye contact is critical when you are face to face and engaged in a personal and intimate conversation. Looking around or looking away at a critical moment can be frustrating and irritating to your partner and ultimately spoil the mood of the moment On the other hand, looking deep into their eyes will make your conversation more personal and more intimate, as well as add strength and reinforcement to anything you might be telling or sharing with them. Fortunately learning to make and maintain eye contact effectively is a skill that can be learned, developed, and improved if you take the time to make a conscious effort. This skill will help you to develop friendships more easily as well as deeper and more personal relationships once mastered.

Show Interest in Their Hobbies

Be supportive, allow them private time to pursue their hobbies but always show interest. You can show interest in many ways. First you can share and participate in their hobby at times, even if it is your less than favorite thing to do. Your willing participation in something they know does not interest you will earn you their love and respect. Too you can show approval by showing financial support, buying them necessary supplies etc. You can also take part by keeping an eye open for events, opportunities, or potential deals related to their hobby. Your approval is necessary, so they can continue to enjoy their past time. If you are negative and discouraging then your mate may give up his or her interests in hopes of pleasing you. A partner with no pursuits or hobbies of their own will most likely become a burden to you. If you are their only remaining interest, they will inevitably appear needy to you.

Ask For Hugs and Kisses

In dating, it seemed to me that asking for a hug or a kiss was a good way to get past the "touch barrier". However in more developed relationships asking for a hug or kiss has a much deeper and more intimate meaning. It expresses the desire of the one asking to bond with the other. It subconsciously expresses a need or want to be closer this person, though not necessarily in a sexual way. I must admit that before doing research for this book, I never understood clearly why the women in my life often asked this question. As a man I always misread this question as an invitation to something more physical. I now understand more clearly the deeper desires that motivate one to ask. So don't be afraid to ask for an unconditional hug, kiss, smile, or some other form of nonsexual touching. You will be amazed at the response, especially if you are a man. Your desire to connect intimately with your partner in a non-sexual way will usually be rewarded tenfold.

Value Their Opinion

There are many ways to value your mate's opinion. Listening attentively to them when they speak is the primary way you can show you value their opinion. You can value their opinion too by using positive body language such as nodding, smiling, or being general agreeable with your facial responses. You can give weight to their considerations by following their suggestions whenever possible. Asking for their opinion also shows you regard their opinion as important. Even when you disagree with their opinion on a particular subject, you can give show respect for their ideas by acknowledging areas of agreement. You should never be disrespectful of their thoughts and feelings by making overly negative, critical, or smart-ass remarks. In successful relationships, the lines of communication should always be open, and both partners should feel they can express their viewpoint without the fear of rejection or humiliation.

Create Love Signals

What is a love signal? It can be anything that you and you partner agree upon from holding pinky fingers to playing footsies under the table. It only has to be understood by you and your mate. In the case of my wife and me, we have several sets of preset love signals and one that constantly changes. Anytime I look at my wife while doing something repetitive three times I am signaling to her those three all-important words – *I love you*. For us this is a fun game since we can constantly change the signal. Today I might walk up to her at work and tap her three times on the shoulder to get her attention. If she notices the signal then I should get one of several preset responses. If she does not notice the signal, then certainly I will get great satisfaction from playing hurt; and naturally I then expect some make up loving. (Wink wink) Of course, if I miss her signal, I am buying a bottle of wine and cooking her dinner tonight. I hope you have as much fun with love signals as we do!

Hold Their Hand

Holding hands is often the first display of affection that a couple shares together, and many times for older couples it is the last. It may seem like only a simple hand gesture, but like love itself, it is very complex in nature and meaning. I'm a firm believer that there is great intangible value in continuing to hold hands with the one you love throughout your lifetime. The act of reaching for their hand clearly communicates to your loved one that you want and desire to be close to them. It is a declaration of your desire to share an intimate bond with them. Not only does holding hands display your affection to your partner, it also displays your commitment to them. It tells the world that the two of you are a couple and that neither of you are available for a relationship with someone else. Holding hands tends to send many positive signals to your mate, some directly and others subliminally. You should always walk through life holding the hand of the one you love.

Nonsexual Touching

Nonsexual touching is one of the most effective ways that you can communicate your love to your partner. It is a powerful sign of affection that will strengthen any relationship. It builds trust between two people, and it deepens the intimacy connection between those people. Walking arm in arm, sitting close to one another, resting your hand on their leg, touching hands across the table, putting your hand on their shoulder, cuddling, snuggling, leaning against them, stroking their hair, caressing their skin, and even holding one another after sex are all examples of nonsexual touching. Relationships normally start with lots of nonsexual contact but often over time this form of loving fades. Sometimes we inadvertently reject this form of touch by being too busy, by being distracting, or by not participating. Refocusing your attention on nonsexual touching will definitely make your mate feel loved by you in any type of relationship.

Publicly Display Affection

Don't worry! I am not suggesting you create a public scene. I understand many people are private by nature and might have reservations about many forms of public affection; however, a public declaration of your love can take on many forms. It can be a basic act of affection like holding hands, sitting close, or a simply kissing hello or good-bye. It can be you speaking proudly of their qualities, talents, or work. Most partners want you to be proud of them and show others you love them, yet at the same time they don't want to be a trophy and they don't want to appear adolescent in nature. Appropriate public displays of affection can be any simple gesture that informs others you love your partner and you don't care who knows. Another example of an acceptable public display of affection might be the use of some pet names, so long as you don't make your mate feel uncomfortable or embarrassed by an unusually private or personal pet name.

Accept Mistakes

Mistakes are going to happen. Don't expect perfection in yourself or your partner and then you won't be disappointed. Many people have trouble being real with themselves because they associate the mistakes they make with either some form of guilt or shame. They often feel that when they admit mistakes that they are somehow less of a person, less of a man, or less of some other unrealistic ideal they are striving for. By accepting the fact that you are going to make mistakes then it becomes easier to accept the mistakes of your mate as well. You must accept and overlook your partner's mistakes if you expect that person to accept yours. The higher the standard that you hold yourself to, the higher standard you tend to hold your mate to. This higher level of accountability tends to be a vicious cycle. So break the cycle and learn to accept your own mistakes so you can show your partner they are loved by overlooking theirs as well.

The Power of Hugs

Hugs are an extremely important component of attachment as they create bonds between two individuals. It is one of the most basic elements of humanity, it knows no international boundaries, it is not limited by language, and it is clearly understood by every culture in the world. Hugs communicate quite eloquently and sublimely that someone is important to you, that you love them, that you need them, that you are attracted to them, that you accept them, that you appreciate them, and that you can be trusted by them. Virginia Satir, a well-known family therapist states, "We need 4 hugs a day for survival. We need 8 hugs a day for maintenance. We need 12 hugs a day for growth." Unfortunately, it may not be possible in your busy lifestyles to hug your loved one 12 times a day, but I do believe it should be possible to embrace them in some combination of 12 times or 12 minutes a day. Do not ever under-estimate the power of hugs in your relationship.

Use the Internet Wisely

Excessive internet usage is one of the top complaints in relationships nowadays. This is why I strongly recommend you limit your internet time to your personal time, not the times you are expected to be together. Improper or overuse of the internet can lead to major issues such as resentment, mistrust, or even jealousy. On the other hand, you can use positive aspects of the internet to enhance your relationship. For example, it can be used to send loves messages, love letters, greeting cards, electronic flowers, etc. If you cannot write poetry or love letters you can search for help. If you cannot think of something to do with your spouse then an internet search can help find ideas, community activities, or local attractions and shows. The internet can either be a good friend or an enemy to your relationship depending on you. By using it wisely to benefit your relationship, you may be rewarded with more time to use it for personal pursuits.

Care for Their Needs

There is an old saying that actions speak louder than words, and this is especially true in relationships. If you want your mate to feel loved then take care of their needs, especially if requested. There are countless things that can be done to make someone feel loved. Cut their nails, polish their shoes, pop their pimples, rub their tired feet, massage their sore muscles, make them coffee, fetch their newspaper, bring them a snack, walk their dog, carry their umbrella, pull out their chair, hold the door for them, and fix their things are examples of ways you can please your partner. It is important to remember that every little action you take or don't take sends a subliminal message. Your actions are usually judged as more important than your words. If you love someone, appreciate them, and their happiness is important to you then you don't need to tell them you love them every five minutes, just show them. Do something for them. Take care of their needs.

King and Queen of Kissing

Though your partner may expect a perfunctory kiss when you come and go, you must avoid doing this in an obligatory way. If daily kissing ritual becomes too routine then it loses its true significance. The feeling you exude when you embrace your partner says a lot about your relationship. This is why you should always kiss them as if you are kissing the hand of royalty or like you are kissing them for the first time again. So take your time and do it right. Show them their true significance to you, each time your lips touch theirs. Embrace them, as you look them in the eye. Stroke their hair, neck and or shoulder. You can warm them up for the big moment with a few gentle kisses to the forehead, cheeks, nose and or chin. Then kiss them like you mean it. Your true passion for them can also be measured by the size of your smile, your enthusiasm to see them, and the fervor of your hug. You will make them feel loved and needed, if you can always kiss them with the passion they deserve.

Display Their Photos

Displaying the photo of your loved one at your work, school, on your phone, or even in your car is a very simple thing to do, but it can have great meaning to some partners in a relationships. Women especially tend to find added comfort and security in this small demonstration of your love. Your photo is often viewed by them as a public declaration of your love and commitment to this person. It shows them that you are proud of them, that they are important to you, and that you appreciate and need them in your life. In the minds of less emotionally secure partners displaying a photo is equivalent to wearing a sign that says "Hands off!!! I am taken". Your willingness to do this voluntarily can give your partner an added sense of security, especially if your mate tends to be the insecure or jealous type. So make that special person in your life feel loved today, display their photo.

Build a Website Together

A family website bonds couples and families more closely together by focusing the attention on the positive aspects of the relationship. It unites people together in a wholesome activity that can be fun and challenging too. It can help to get your children more involved in family activities, as nowadays children often know more about computers than their parents. It demonstrates pride in each other and in each other's accomplishments by serving as an archive for family photos and a showcase for individual and family accomplishments. It helps a family stay connected and informed of important events; especially if in-laws live in distant places or if older children are already off to school or living on their own. It can also lead to families getting closer or reconnecting with extended family members such as aunts, uncles, cousins, nieces, and nephews. I truly hope you will not miss out on this wonderful opportunity to draw closer to your loved ones.

Whisper In Their Ear

To many people, especially some ladies, sharing a few heartfelt whisperings can have greater meaning than even an expensive gift. You don't have to be a poet to make someone feel special and cherished, just be yourself and say what you feel in your own heartfelt words. The more authentic and sincere your words sound the greater the significance and impact they will have to your partner. Though it is always better not to use borrowed words and quoted lines, it does not hurt to plan ahead a little. Put together in your mind three or four main ideas or points that you want to cover, but don't over think or over plan your exact wording, as it is best not to worry too much or try to memorize some big long speech. When the time is appropriate you want your words to sound natural and to be your own. Trust me on this one, when done correctly, you will not only be whispering into their ear you will also be whispering into their heart and soul too.

Importance of Secrets

Secrets bond people together. Sharing secrets with someone is an indication of friendship and trust, so sharing secrets together from your mutual friends and family can help unite you and your loved one together as a couple. In many cases, this "us against the world" mentality can strengthen the bonds of your relationship. Though sharing secrets from others can be a unifying force in your relationship there may also times when it is best to keep an occasional secret from your partner. In a perfect and ideal world we would never keep secrets from our life partner, but unfortunately there are some secrets that may be best buried and forgotten as they would cause our loved one and our relationship irreparable harm. In these rare situations, where you may have faltered significantly, keeping a secret may still be advisable. A few less meaningful secrets can also keep your mate intrigued and interested in learning more and more about you.

Don't Be Owned By Your Possessions

You may think you own your possessions, but the reality is they also own you. Everything you possess must be cleaned, maintained, repaired, stored, protected, insured, or cared for in one manner or another. This requires a huge investment of your time, money, and energy. Unless you are one of the world's ultra-rich and can easily afford to pay others to do all of this for you, then the more time you dedicate to your possessions the less time you have to devote to your relationships. If you find yourself stressing over a lack of time, always working to make one more payment, or always ignoring your loved ones then probably it is time for you to regain control of your life. Simplify your life by taking inventory of what is truly important to you. Selling off a few possessions can often relieve stress, buy back time, and improve the overall quality of your relationship.

Sleeping Closely

If you think the way you sleep with someone is insignificant then you are surely misjudging the power that the subconscious mind has on your relationship. The emotional attachment or detachment that is felt, especially in the case of women, changes dramatically by the amount of physical contact you maintain with them at night. Sleeping positions are often an exact reflection of the true status of your relationship. The farther apart you sleep, the directions you face, and the amount of body contact are all very telling signs when it comes to evaluating your relationship. The way you fall asleep and wake up have a profound effect on the subconscious perceptions of your mate. It may be impossible to sleep embraced all night but your partner will feel a stronger attachment if you maintain as much contact as possible. Nightly and morning embraces, holding hands, a hand on their back or shoulder, legs intertwined, and your desire to lay close all make your spouse feel loved subconsciously.

Compliment Your Mate

Compliments are usually most effective when kept simple. If a compliment is too wordy or too perfect then it may come off sounding as if it was preplanned. If your compliment is too complicated or over the top then your loved one may doubt your authenticity or suspect your motives. A compliment is most effective at a time when you have nothing to gain. If the timing of a compliment is appropriate you can also make your compliment in a public place or discussion, so long as you word the compliment in a manner that does not make it seem like you are trying to attract attention to yourself. Compliments made publicly in front of others often have a more powerful effect. Honest heartfelt compliments are totally free so you can definitely afford to participate. Every genuine compliment you make to your mate is like saying I love you in a different way. So reach out and touch your loved one's heart by sharing a heartfelt compliment with them today.

Defend Your Partner

You should always be seen as a protector of the honor and reputation of your partner. If anyone disrespects your mate you must be seen as having their back at all times. This is especially true in the case of your own parents, siblings, and children you might have from a previous relationship. If any of your family has a negative attitude towards your mate, it is imperative that you defend your mate whether they are right or wrong from frontal attacks. There probably will be times when your family and your mate will encounter issues. It is your responsibility to control your family if they act inappropriately. Direct attacks, sarcasm, and disparaging remarks should not be overlooked or tolerated. The proper boundaries of respect must be maintained. Any attack on your mate is an attack on your relationship too. Failure to see this important association will leave your mate feeling your relationship with them is secondary to your relationship with the attacker.

Give Unexpected Gifts

In reality it is not the unexpected gift that will usually impress. It is the thought and meaning behind the gift that tends to melt the other's heart. Giving an unexpected gift is a random act of love that will remind your partner that they are special and important to you every day of the year. It shows your loved one you are thinking about them, even when you are away. It lets them know that they are important to you, and it reinforces the fact that you truly want to make them feel loved and happy. Unexpected gifts can also be a great way to say thank you and show your mate that you do not take for granted all the small things they do for you, when you use an unexpected gift to thank them for some small thing that they frequently do for you. For example, when presenting the gift, you can thank them for the wonderful meal that they had ready for you when you arrived home last night or you can thank them for being a good parent to your children.

Simplify Life Together

Life gets cluttered so every couple years I recommend that you sit down together and find ways to simplify your life. This must be a joint project. It is human nature to bite off more than we can chew, to get distracted from what is most important, and to change our focus; so you should remove unnecessary possessions from your life as this removes stress. Cleaning out your house and having a garage sale gets rid of unused belongings that require time, energy, and money to maintain. You should also simplify your finances. Look for unnecessary expenditures and items that may no longer be as needed as you once thought. It is amazing how much time you can save by paying bills electronically. Use automatic deposit to a safe account, and then transfer sufficient funds to another account for automated payments online of your basic bills. Many programs allow payment by confirmation only. The time and energy you save simplifying your life can then be devoted to your loved ones.

Accept Growth and Change

As creatures of habit, sometimes it is very difficult thing to watch your mate grow and change. This is especially true if their growth or maturing may somehow affect your own comfort level in the relationship. Once you recognize that a change is occurring, it is important to recognize the need to check and adjust your own perceptions and outlook. Your attitude is the single most important element in successfully accepting changes as they occur. Through open-minded reflection you may need to remind yourself that change is inevitable and that by accepting the change willingly you are allowing your mate to fulfill their own dreams or reach their own potential. Keep in mind that your acceptance and approval will truly be an unselfish display of your love and affection for your mate. At times it can be helpful to remind yourself of all changes that your life partner has had to adjust to as you previously matured in your relationship with them.

Respect Private Time

There are two forms of private time that you need to respect that will make your partner feel loved - private time together and private time apart. Private time together is regular times designated as together time such as after a certain hour each evening. If agreements have been made for private time together, then you must learn to say no to friends, work, or other invading forces and respect this time. Private time apart must also be respected. Most often in a relationship one mate needs more private time apart than other. If you happen to be the more dependent one in the relationship it can be somewhat difficult to accept your partner's more independent attitudes. If you feel anger, depression, or other negative feelings when they need time alone then you must objectively examine yourself to determine the true root of the problem or your insecurities. You must keep in mind that it is an act of love to allow and trust your mate to have their private time alone or with their friends.

Chapter Five: 25 Ways To Avoid Unnecessary Conflicts

Count to Ten

Any fool can start a quarrel, so always take a deep breath and count to ten before responding to something that has enraged you. Learning to control your tongue is not as simple as it might seem. It may take years of practice, but if you make a conscious effort it can be done. Mental preparation is the major key to success with this strategy. You should have some action or words in mind that you will employ the next time you are angered. For smaller issues I try to diffuse the situation with humor, so I grab my balls and act like my wife just kicked me in the nuts. When I find myself very upset I tell her I love her too much to respond immediately to those hurtful words. With forethought you can find soft words and ways that convey your displeasure yet diffuse the situation until you are better able to discuss it later. Learning self-control prevents small arguments from escalating into major confrontations, and it also gives you less to apologize for later if you are the one in the wrong.

Don't Vent, Don't Rant & Rave

Ranting and raving is unproductive and unacceptable behavior. It may make you feel better momentarily, but in the end it is most likely to harm a relationship more than heal it. Venting normally leads to actions that are forbidden in successful relationships such as pointing out faults, blaming your partner, and revisiting old issues. Every time you lose self-control you may inadvertently be giving your partner permission to do the same on another occasion depending on their nature and character. Every time you lose control you may escalate the current issue into an all-out battle as ranting and raving normally leads to retaliation. Every time you lose control you are very likely to say things that you will regret later. These un-retractable words can build resentment and walls in your relationship, as well as test your loved one's ability to forgive and forget. This is why you should never rant and rave. It is always best to deal with one issue at a time as patiently as possible.

Don't Flirt With Others

Flirting while involved in a relationship is a self-destructive habit that undermines your relationship. It will cause your partner to feel offended or disrespected, and almost always leads to feelings of jealousy and insecurity. Inevitably flirting will lead to conflict and hurt feelings or even acts of desperation if your partner decides to leave the relationship or take revenge with some other form of cheating. If you find yourself flirting uncontrollable you definitely should examine yourself and your own motives thoroughly. You should ask yourself these questions: Do you feel a need to make your partner jealous or to get them to pay attention to you? Are you seeking appreciation and love from others that you are not getting from your partner? Are you flirting to overcome feelings of low self-esteem and self-worth? By finding the true cause of your behavior, you can then hopefully find a constructive cure to this self-sabotaging behavior of yours.

Turn the Other Cheek

Your mate does not need to slap you literally for you to turn the other cheek. Figuratively speaking every time they act aggressively, whether it is through verbal assault or emotional pain, you must be the better person and offer them your other cheek. By responding to aggression with a non-aggressive response, you will deescalate the current conflict and hopefully teach them the proper ways to deal with their ill feelings and future conflicts. When they are insensitive or deliberately trying to hurt your feelings, your response with kindness and concern will leave them feeling ashamed of their brutality. Only a totally ruthless person can assault someone who does not defend themselves. Most aggression is behavior that was learned previously in other dysfunctional relationships. Relationships can be quite challenging, especially if either or both partners have histories of dysfunctional relationships in their family backgrounds. Break the cycle of aggression, by turning the other cheek.

Don't Blame Each Other

Couples need to accept the fact that there are going to be differences of opinions. No one has to be right thus making the other person wrong. Not everything is black and white. Even in cases where one person is obviously at fault, blaming that person will only make them defensive and uncooperative. Thus it is imperative to focus on the problem in front of you and resolving it together, not on who is to blame. Most often if you focus on who is to blame you will miss the opportunity to resolve the issue quickly and calmly. It is also important in every confrontation that you remain positive, that you express your concerns and viewpoint in a manner that is not accusatory, and that you work towards a peaceful and hopefully permanent resolution. In fact, whenever possible, openly accept blame for whatever you may have done wrong. By accepting your fair share of the blame but never giving it, you will demonstrate a willingness to resolve any issue peacefully.

Avoid Pet Peeve Problems

Most pet peeves are caused by laziness or by undervaluing their importance to your loved one. I define a pet peeve as a minor annoyance, so this does not refer to any major or inappropriate behaviors such as telling lies or cheating on your mate. Instead, we are discussing things like closing the cupboards, putting things away, and putting down the toilet seat. Here are some rules for preventing pet peeves from becoming a major issue in your relationship: 1. Pet peeves caused by laziness should never happen. 2. Pet peeves caused by undervaluing their importance should be discussed, BUT never in the middle of argument. 3. If pet peeves cannot be stopped then they can be traded off. (Example: I can leave the toilet seat up if you can leave the cupboard doors open.) This can be fun, if you think of all the possibilities. When all the cupboards are open, you will definitely know why. 4. If you have more than 10 pet peeves, you are too sensitive!!!

Be Open-minded

To avoid unnecessary conflict in your relationship it is important that you be open to new thoughts, suggestions, ideas, and even to criticism. Aristotle said, "It is the mark of an educated mind to be able to entertain a thought without accepting it." It is human nature to be defensive and always want to be right. Yet if you can learn to be objective and not to reject criticism easily then you allow yourself and your relationship the chance to grow and blossom. An open mind will also allow you to interact with your partner without judging them or their intentions, encouraging them to build greater levels of trust and intimacy with you. If you listen attentively to criticism you definitely will gain more of their respect and confidence, and even though you may disagree at the time usually later you will find some value in what they have said. Be open to new ideas, just because you did not think of something does not mean it has no value.

Be a Peacemaker

Never take the offensive position, always seek peace. Remember - marriage is supposed to be a team sport not a war, not a battle of the sexes, and not a battle for control of the universe. To be a successful peacemaker in your relationship requires advanced forethought and mental resolution on your part. If you are not committed to making peace it may be easy for your loved one to provoke you into a battle, especially if they are not as committed to the peace process as you. You must be prepared to remain positive, objective, and empathetic as you strive to reach a mutually beneficial resolution. You must be prepared to ignore any false or provocative accusations and actions as your partner tries to ensnare you with their anger or lead you into a battle no one wins. Listening attentively is the best weapon of a peacemaker, as the warmonger will usually calm down or tire if you can remain positive, optimistic and willing to make peace.

Choose Your Battles Wisely

Is it really worth sleeping on couch because you prefer the mustard in the cupboard and the wife prefers the mustard in the refrigerator? Are all the tears, anger, and long lasting resentment really justifiable for 79 cents? Would not it be better just to buy two bottles of mustard – one for the cupboard and one for the refrigerator? Sometimes we can lose sight of the correct perspective on things, as it is extremely easy to get caught up in the battle for power and control or in a fight to determine who is right and wrong. This is why it is important for you to choose your battles wisely. Should not all this emotional pain and struggling be saved for some other battle that truly has some significant meaning to you. Also if you learn to choose your battles more wisely, you will learn to be far more effective in winning those battles that truly are important to you. The more battles that you have for petty reasons, the more likely your partner is to battle you for power and control over everything little thing in your life.

Be Willing to Negotiate

In relationships you create the couple you want to be through negotiation, followed by compromise. You need to have good will and faith in each other to be able to negotiate and renegotiate your relationship as it grows and changes over time. To keep communication open you must be flexible and willing to negotiate with an open mind. Your partner will not have the confidence and trust to share their true feelings and needs with you if you are closed minded and unwilling to negotiate. If your partner is shut out of negotiations or their needs are overlooked continuously then resentment and walls will develop over time in your relationship. Thus the long term health and depth of true intimacy in your relationship is directly related to your willingness to negotiate and compromise. Often times the stronger personality in the relationship will win the short term battles, but ultimately the relationship suffers inevitable harm if both parties cannot negotiate equitably in good faith.

Never Omit the Truth

I know we covered lying before, but since many people try to convince themselves that omitting facts is not the same as lying I want to be very clear on this - omitting the truth is lying! That is why our courts swear us in the way they do during a trial. You pledge to tell the truth (no lies), the *whole* truth (no omitting), and nothing but the truth (no exaggerating, minimizing, justifying, etc.) Anything less than the *whole* truth is only partially true. If something is only partially true then it must also be partially false. The part that is partially false is the lie, the part that tends to always get omitted. If you make a mistake you need to own it as soon as possible. It is always far worse for your mate to uncover the *whole* truth on their own. Trust is one of the cornerstones of your relationship. If your mate loses trust in you, then your relationship is doomed. The truth always finds a way to be discovered, so avoid conflict by always telling the *whole* truth every time.

Don't Procrastinate

Procrastination often shifts the burdens of responsibility onto your mate. Also by constantly putting off your loved one and their needs, your bad habit makes them feel less important. Over time these shifted responsibilities and feelings of neglect will have stressful effects on your relationship, often causing resentment to build. Procrastination also causes you feel to feel additional stress and anxiety too, as you strive to meet mandatory deadlines. If this negative energy is inadvertently refocused onto your partner, as is often the case, this will compound the damage being done to your relationship. Procrastinators often suffer from lower levels of self-esteem and higher levels of depression. These negative symptoms of procrastination are also detrimental and undermining to relationships over time. So be smart, and avoid many unnecessary problems. Create greater love and harmony in your relationship, by never procrastinating.

Keep Your Commitments

To avoid conflict, you must never take your commitments too lightly or promise more than you can deliver. When you make a promise, whether small or large, you must keep the promise. It's imperative that you view your word as the cornerstone of your personal integrity and honor; in the same manner your mate probably views your word and assurances. The difficulty of keeping a promise may sometimes be more than you expect, but the cost of breaking promises can be even higher. Broken promises lead to instant conflict, as your loved one feels hurt and disappointed. Worse than this, they cause walls to build in your relationship, as mistrust and resentments cause distance between you and them emotionally. Too many unfulfilled pledges will result in other negative feelings and attitudes developing towards you. Their loss of faith in you can even lead to the end of the relationship. So be wise, and only make promises you can keep.

Don't Over Analyze

Analysis is a normal human response, but sometimes enough is enough. You can ruin a relationship worrying and stressing over the deeper meaning of ever small word and action. If you are not inclined to accept things at face value, it might indicate you have feelings of insecurity about yourself, your partner, or your relationship. It might also be an indicator that you yourself are less than honest with own your words and feelings at times. If you have a tendency to over-analyze then you should seek a resolution to the deeper causes of this destructive and obsessive behavior. When not dealt with properly, over-analyzing is often a self-fulfilling prophecy. The fear of rejection leads to over-analyzing, as you look for evidence that your partner is emotionally detaching from you. The over-analyzing leads to disputes, ultimately driving the person away from you emotionally. This then causes your unfounded fears to come true. So be smart and be balanced, don't over-analyze everything.

Avoid Being Under the Influence

Just like cars and alcohol is a bad mix, so is love and alcohol. An occasional drink can be enjoyable and relaxing, but consistent and or heaving drinking has clear associations with dysfunctional families and failed relationships. Alcohol has been clearly linked with lowered inhibitions and a reduced ability of the drinker to evaluate the consequences of their behavior. If you drink, lack of self-control can destroy your relationship in countless ways. Infidelity, aggression, and conflict are just to name a few. Studies indicate that the higher your level of dependence on alcohol the higher the level of dysfunction will be in your relationships. Research on average proves that every extra drink per day adds greater stress and increases the likelihood and possibility that your actions will seriously harm your relationship. Thus you should always try to drink the least amount possible, as you try to avoid conflict in your life relationships.

Resolve Small Issues Promptly

Avoiding conflict resolution is actually worse than facing your fear of it. Small problems can quickly grow bigger. Simple issues can often leave permanent scars on your relationship as resentment and walls build over time when things are not resolved quickly. If you have experienced conflict in unhealthy relationships then you may find conflict more threatening to you than it really is. In reality there is nothing to fear about conflict. It is a natural and inevitable part of all relationships. When resolved quickly and in a healthy way, conflict increases your understanding of yourself and your partner. It can even build trust and a greater depth of love when both parties involved can see and understand the others commitment to the relationship. So when small issues develop don't be afraid to resolve them quickly, as you might even miss an opportunity to strengthen the bonds of your relationship.

Avoid Unilateral Decisions

Even if your partner seems to allow you to make unilateral decisions you must be careful not to abuse this privilege. Their submission may come with a price – long term resentment. When a unilateral decision is imposed on the other party in a relationship, the result may be of questionable value and duration. Your partner may be agreeing for a variety of reasons. If they are only agreeing to keep the peace temporarily or to avoid immediate conflict then inevitably in time this issue will be revisited. Once sufficient anger and resentment has built and they have reached their boiling point your unilateral decisions may come back to haunt you.. This is why it is always best to include your loved one's input into all your major decisions. If you sense they are going along reluctantly then you need to weigh the value of your decision against the long-term health of your relationship. It may be best to compromise or concede now then end up in major conflict later.

Don't Forget Crucial Dates

Whatever you do, don't dare forget those crucial dates. Most people when asked believe that remembering dates is a vital expression of love. Since women most often have an uncanny ability to recall dates and are much more likely to feel hurt if someone forgets, I hope every man will read this section twice. Remembering your anniversary and important birthdays makes your loved one feel special. It also reinforces in their mind that your relationship with them is meaningful to you. If you have a tendency to forget dates then don't hesitate to use your computer or phone to remind you. It is easy to setup alarms and reminders on these devices. I strongly recommend you set at least two alarms for each date. Set one a few days in advance to allow you time to prepare a gift, flowers, or whatever is appropriate. The other should be set for the morning of the event, just in case you are still not prepared for some forgetful reason.

Don't Push Their Buttons

Most of the frustration and anger in a relationship can be avoided. The key is to learn and understand the emotional triggers that we all possess. If you understand your own emotional triggers, your partner cannot use them against you unwittingly. You must learn theirs too, so you can be emotional supportive and constructive. Most likely you already know your partner well enough to know what buttons not to push. If your relationship is new, it is important to learn their triggers and their limits as soon as possible. Using their weaknesses against them is a form of disrespect, so please remember to fight fairly. Never pull their triggers intentionally, just to get back at them. They are likely to remember this for a long long time if they discover your indiscretion. Don't push their buttons or use their weaknesses against them for petty revenge. Instead, as a loving and supportive partner, use this valuable information to prevent and minimize conflicts when they occur.

Remember to Forget

How good you are at quickly forgetting negative thoughts and feelings from your conscious mind can have a direct impact on preventing unnecessary conflicts in your current relationship. If you are not careful, it is possible to carry forward destructive feelings towards your partner because of some incident or other. Over time these ill feelings you lug with you from previous setbacks, letdowns and disappointments can build into larger issues. Anger, animosity, resentment, depression, and other negative emotions can be dramatically reduced by learning to forget. Chronic hostility towards your mate or constantly recalling and reminding your partner of past offenses are evidences that you may not have let go and forgotten completely. If you find yourself unable to let go or forget, it can help to look at your own culpability in the original issue. If this does resolve it in your mind, then it may be best to talk about your feelings again with your mate.

Apologize and Reassure

Apologizing is not the easiest thing to do, but when we err it is essential. By taking responsibility for your mistakes you express your desire to be better and to keep trying to please your mate. In a good apology you should admit to what you did wrong, tell your partner why it was wrong, and reassure them it won't happen again. At times you may not feel that you were completely wrong, but trying to meet them halfway with a limited apology will demonstrate good faith and hopefully help your loved one to overcome any hurt feelings. In every relationship there are times when both partners owe the other an apology at the same time. In this situation, you should not be too proud to be the first one to apologize. Your willingness to admit your own culpability will help to resolve the issue at hand and demonstrates your commitment to the relationship. It will make you feel better, and ultimately will be the first step on the way to a happy reconciliation.

Leave Anger Behind

Anger is a natural part of every relationship, but anger can only be destructive to your relationship. So stay calm and speak in a normal voice, as a self-centered display of anger is unproductive. Losing control of your temper will only aggravate the problem or cause it to escalate. Since you spend so much time together and you know your mate's shortcomings so well, it is very natural to become critical and short-tempered with them. It becomes easy to blame him or her for making your life difficult or uncomfortable. Realistically anger is a selfish emotion that is complete opposed to the principles of love. If you allow anger to grow then inevitably you are allowing your love to die. I heard it said once that every opportunity to develop anger is also an opportunity to develop patience. This is why you must constantly re-evaluate your own attitudes towards your partner and your relationship, as true love knows no anger.

Never Make Threats

Threats tend to be counterproductive and are always perceived in a negative manner. Threats often send the wrong signal to your mate. For example, a threat to leave tends to say I do not love you anymore, instead of I love you but I think you are acting selfishly. A skillful negotiator will seldom use a threat, since they normally lead to counter threats and create negative feelings that destroy the relationship and any possibility of negotiation. Most threats come from a person with a perceived sense of power. Since most relationships have some ongoing battle for control, a threat is often viewed as an attempt to grab power or a flexing of existing power. To avoid escalating a conflict, it is better to request to discuss or negotiate whatever issue happens to be stirring up things at the moment. By approaching your partner in a more positive manner, their response will likely be more positive in nature too. This way you will not stir up additional conflict.

Discuss Finances Together

Money cannot buy love, but it absolutely can rip it apart. This is why you must always be honest and communicative about your financial situation. Differences in financial goals, spending habits, and even in the importance of individual purchases can cause major conflicts. Depending on your own circumstances, you should have weekly or monthly discussions about developing financial goals and budgets together. Discussing money matters is often extremely difficult for couples, as money is tied directly to our individual emotional needs. Individually we use money to express our emotional needs like security, independence, self-esteem, status, or power and control. Thus whenever you discuss money, it is important that each person put aside their emotions and remember to remain rational. Both parties need to always be positive and honest, keeping in mind their partner's emotional and financial needs, as well as their own.

Don't Be Condescending

When you look at yourself objectively, do you see yourself acting superior or treating your mate in a condescending manner? This can be a learned behavior from a poor role model or parent or it can come from a deeper rooted inferiority complex. Either way you must work on improvement in this critical area, as such people have a much lower success rate in long term relationships. On the other hand, if you are dealing with a condescending person, it is important that you be somewhat accepting of their character flaw. You should try to deal with the insecurities behind the attitude, but not at the moment they are showing you their worst side. You should be prepared when conflicts occur to overlook their poor attitude as much as possible and deal with the current issue at hand. Don't take their remarks too personally, yet it is important to let the person know that there are boundaries to their behavior while staying calm.

Chapter Six: 20 Plus Ways To Resolve Differences Peacefully

Let Them Speak

Good relationships are always coauthored by both parties, so listening to your loved one's opinions and viewpoints is imperative in conflict resolution. Listening to their complaints and criticisms will make them more receptive to listening to your side of the issue when you feel you have been wronged. Listening attentively is also a sign of respect and displays your willingness to compromise and negotiate a reasonable solution to the issue in front of you. Try to hear out their whole complaint before responding, as the root of the problem is often not the first thing said and sometimes never even mentioned. Even when you may totally disagree you can always state, "Well that's an interesting viewpoint" and allow them to continue. If you have a tendency to interrupt or cut them off they will inevitably feel you are overlooking or minimizing their concerns. Often in conflicts just allowing the other to speak freely will help to calm the situation by letting them vent their feelings a little.

A Soft Answer Turns Away Wrath

There are wise words in a good book that says, "a soft answer can turn away wrath," and "good words make a heart glad." The truth is it takes two to fight. A wise person can guide a potential argument into constructive resolution of conflict by mentally preparation. When verbally attacked, your first response will determine if the battle rages on or if rational heads will prevail. It really makes no difference if their accusation and or their approach to conflict are totally wrong. Even when falsely attacked aggressively, you can still say something like, "Wow, I can see that I have upset you, I would never do that on purpose. I hope we can resolve this." By avoiding the word "you" they will not feel threatened. By using the word "I" you show your willingness to participate. The word "we' will remind them this should be about "us and we" and not you or I. Having deflected their aggression, you can now begin to calmly and with unity resolve whatever issues exist one by one.

Empathy Creates "Us"

Normally in a conflict your partner will be a mirror of your own attitude. If you are verbally aggressive, narcissistic, and accusatory in nature then they will try to match or out do you. Likewise, if you are concerned and empathetic of their viewpoint, they will tend to be reasonable and willing to compromise when they feel you are acting fairly and unselfishly. Your empathy for your partner will help create the "us and we" experience that is needed to make a couple strive for the couple's mutual benefit. If you are self-centered and unconcerned about your loved one's feelings, wants, and needs - then you will create a "me versus you" attitude in your relations. The "me versus you" scenario inevitably leads to battles of who is right or wrong and battles for the control of power. Empathy is fundamentally an emotional experience; but in relationships it is also a skill that can be developed, enhanced, and perfected when you make a conscious effort to do so.

Refuse To Be Provoked

Are you easily provoked? Does your partner deliberately push your buttons sometimes? Well don't forget it takes two people to fight, so you must plan in advance to be the better person. If you truly love your partner, it is important to remember that arguments can escalate if neither person has self-control. This can often badly damage a relationship, even destroy it completely, so you must give a lot of forethought to this subject. Be mentally prepared to engage your battle plan when your mate might try to provoke you. If you have the same arguments and the same outcome repeatedly, this is good technique to help stop recycling the same old issue(s) over and over again. Don't be afraid to tell your loved one directly that you love them too much to have this same battle again. Usually when you minimize a problem for the sake of love then your partner is willing to do the same. Love and cooperation are really quite contagious experiences.

Ask Questions

Questions normally will deescalate a situation for many reasons. First, it is difficult for your mate to continue an argument if you do not give them any negative or contradictory responses. The longer they are allowed to speak the more they are venting their own feelings and frustrations. Also the person being asked a question must momentarily stop arguing to contemplate their answer. By being mentally prepared in advance to ask questions and then not interrupt, you will gain a complete understanding of their side of the issue. It is very difficult to even discuss an issue if the other person is still upset or if you respond prematurely and don't address their main concern. They will be much more interested in hearing your viewpoint after they have expressed their own. Questions can also be a good way to generate thought and empathy for your viewpoint if you feel you have been wronged. So don't be drawn into an argument too quickly, just ask questions in a concerned manner.

Control Tone and Volume

Have you ever tried to argue with someone who remains calm and in control? It is a very difficult thing to do. Controlling your tone and volume puts you in charge. There are two important keys to being successful. First, you must be mentally prepared in advance to remain completely calm. Secondly, you must not appear to be trying to frustrate your partner by ignoring or minimizing their complaint, so ask questions about their concerns. Many couples inadvertently allow conflicts to escalate by trying to out-duel their partner. By controlling the tone and volume of your voice you can keep the argument limited and focused on the real issue at hand. Tone and volume will keep the situation in check, giving you the opportunity to remind your partner that you love them and you only want to find a compromise or resolution to the ongoing conflict. If you speak softly with a loving and empathetic tone it will be very difficult for your mate to remain angry and uncooperative for very long.

Speak in the "I"

When discussing issues or confronting your partner, you should avoid using the word *you*. The word *you* is often interpreted as an accusation, and will put your partner into a defensive mode. They are much less likely to listen objectively to your complaint or your side of the issue if they feel they are under attack. Always use the word *I* instead. Don't say, "*You* make me angry." Instead you should say, "*I* feel angry. " By speaking in the first person tense you can convey your thoughts, feelings, and/or pain in a manner that is less aggressive and threatening to your spouse. They will be much more likely to deal with the conflict in a constructive manner. When your partner is confronting you I strongly recommend that you try never to be defensive, even if their choice of words is not as careful as your own. If you speak in the "*I*", but understand and tolerate their use of the word "*you*", then hopefully you will be able to deal with confrontations and conflicts in a better manner.

Breathe and Pause

One of the best techniques to control an argument is to take a deep breaths and then to pause after each breath. Your pause has several purposes. First, it allows the deep breaths you took a chance to work. A deep breath will help you to relax as it counteracts the adrenaline that starting flowing when you began to feel upset and stressed. Pausing will help to calm you down and will trigger a relaxation response in your brain. The more relaxed you can remain the more clearly you think. The second purpose of pausing is to slow down the arguing process. The faster an argument goes the louder voices tend to get and the more it tends to escalate. The third purpose of pausing is to allow your partner a chance to vent a little. Often just letting them speak their mind a little can calm an argument down. However, the most important reason to pause is to give yourself a moment to choose your words carefully. Remember a soft answer can turn way wrath.

Pray Together

Praying together unites people in one purpose, so what could be better for a troubled relationship? Prayer will always calm a situation as you humble yourselves to your greater God and put the importance on something greater than yourselves When a couple, or even a family, turns to God in prayer their stress and anger is replaced with the hope and comfort of God's spirit as they give their burdens to him. Prayer often brings the size of the conflict into better perspective too. Prayer will help to remind those involved in the conflict that no one is perfect and everyone needs divine guidance and wisdom. It will also remind you of the principles of your god too. Praying openly for forgiveness displays your heartfelt desire to do what is right and reminds your partner that you are trying to please them. Praying for strength and endurance displays your commitment to your spouse and reminds them that you are committed long-term to your relationship with them.

Spiritual Counseling

Family counseling through your local religious group is often a valuable opportunity for couples to learn or be reminded of the qualities, strategies, skills, and Godly principles they need to manage life together in a healthy way. Most religions offer some type of family counseling when requested. This form of spiritual counseling is often a good solution for couples who attend a church on a regular basis, as both mates will usually have trust and confidence in their Church leaders already and may feel more comfortable asking for help there than with a stranger. You can often resolve issues much faster through a local group, as they will already have extensive knowledge of your personalities and personal lives that can help them guide you quickly to workable solutions in your particular relationship. Couples who are embarrassed or hesitant to seek help at their local church can try seeking counseling online. Most religion groups offer some form of online help if you look there.

Fight Fairly

Unfortunately conflict and confrontation are going to inevitably occur in every relationship at some point in time, so it important to fight fairly. Each couple should make a set of "fight rules". These should be discussed in advance, but never in the middle of another argument. Here some suggestions that I recommend. Never fight in front of the kids, visiting family, or guests. Never try to hurt your loved one, remember you are supposed to be on the same team and working for the good of your relationship. Always act and speak in the same manner you want them to treat you. Never be insulting or humiliating. Always avoid sarcasm and cynicism. Try not to act superior or condescending. Remember to leave past issues in the past, as they should have been forgiven and forgotten already. Honor all agreements regarding rule of conduct and conflict resolution. Don't bully, push, poke, intimidate, or threaten. Physical aggression is totally unacceptable behavior.

Diffuse Their Anger

An argument is like a pot of water coming to a boil. You should not wait for it to boil over before you turn the heat down, right? When you notice a little excess heat in your conversation, you must take action. When angered by someone we often don't care enough to prevent them from boiling over, especially if we feel they are wrong, they attacked us in some form, or they approached us in a negative manner. The truth is diffusing their anger will most likely benefit yourself too, as these arguments always end with both parties feeling awful anyway. So forget right and wrong; be the better person and turn the heat down. It does not matter who turned it up, fix the problem before you get burned too. Then you can deal with all the issues later when cooler heads prevail. Be empathetic, hug them, ask questions, listen attentively and nod, allow them to vent, admit fault when wrong, and don't be defensive (even when right) are all ways to diffuse their anger.

Give True Forgiveness

To get forgiveness, you must also give it freely. True forgiveness is a three step process. First, you must forgive your loved one for whatever they did. Second, you must learn to let go of any ill feelings or emotional pain you have suffered. This second step is the most difficult, and it often takes time to accomplish completely. This can be especially true if you feel your partner is not taking their responsibilities seriously or if their transgression is of a serious nature. Then last but not least you must forget, never bringing up this issue again when angered by something else. True forgiveness can be a very difficult process, especially if you are hanging on to the need to be right, the desire for revenge, anger, other unexpressed resentments, or an inability to let go of some fear. It is important to remember that forgiveness is 100% your responsibility once you have decided to offer it. Anything less than true forgiveness on your part will cause the issue to resurface repeatedly.

Avoid Sarcasm

Sarcasm, when you are angry, is disrespectful and demeaning. It is an ugly beast, and it should be avoided like the plague. In relationships it is negative and uncooperative by nature, and it should be reserved for humor only. Even in humor, it should never be aimed at your mate. Your humor may leave your mate wondering if there is a little truth in your words. Sarcasm can cause or feed your partner's insecurities and undermine the overall trust in your relationship. This is why I recommend that sarcasm only be directed at yourself, at others, or at yourselves as a couple; but never individually at your partner. Most definitions of sarcasm have some reference to "cutting remark". The brilliance of sarcasm is normally in this cutting aspect. Sarcasm is usually designed to cut down one person, making the other person feels superior. On the other hand, relationships are supposed to be constructive and uniting. Avoid sarcasm, and stay united as one.

Take Responsibility

There is an old saying, "Confession is good for the soul." However, in the case of relationships, your confession is also good for your partner's soul as well as your own. Taking responsibility for your actions is an important step in allowing your partner to let go of and forget your shortcomings. If you refuse to accept blame when it is squarely yours, there is a strong possibility your partner will feel you are quietly shifting the blame to them. They also might worry that events will repeat themselves, if they feel you do not understand the importance of their grievance or recognize your mistake. Ideally, in a perfect relationship, there is no need for right and wrong, as we strive for mutual happiness. However, in reality, it is human nature to need occasional validation, to know we are right. This makes it easier for your partner to let go, and prevents walls of resentment from building in your relationship. So take responsibility for your mistakes, admit it when you are wrong.

Follow Rules of Conduct

Everyone has different levels of acceptance and tolerance. Everyone has different emotional triggers and pet peeves that should be protected by rules of conduct. These guidelines like your fight rules need to be mutually agreed upon and determined in advanced, not in the middle of another argument. Unlike fight rules, these rules of conduct can include anything preventative that will help your relationship run more smoothly day to day and anything that will help you to minimize and resolve conflicts more quickly or peacefully. It is especially imperative during times of disagreement that these rules are followed willingly. If either partner needs to offer the other a friendly reminder, it is important not to take offense. These guidelines have been predetermined to help resolve just such situations before a major conflict erupts. Like a good relationship, your rules of conduct will be reached though communication, negotiation, and compromise.

Never Withhold Sex

No issue can ever be successfully resolved by withholding sex. Withholding sex is a cruel and selfish act that only builds resentment and walls in a relationship. In fact withholding sex often destroys a relationship as the deprived person views this serious transgression as a sign that you want to be in total control or a sign that you are unwilling to negotiate. Withholding sex may lead your partner to desperate acts, such as infidelity or abandoning the relationship altogether. You should always try to resolve arguments before bedtime whenever possible. By doing this you will be careful not to attribute any negative feelings or motives to the most intimate quarters of your life. The bedroom should always remain a safe haven for a couple's intimacy. After a conflict men should try to understand that a woman may take a moment longer than a man to feel the desire for sex again, while women must try to understand the man's ability to forgive and forget faster.

Buy a Solution

Sometimes you find yourselves fighting over the same minor issues repeatedly. For example, your mate may not like that you throw your jacket on the couch when you come home or that you put your feet up on the end table when you watch TV. These small fights over seemingly trivial things can frequently ruin an evening. Such annoyances often accumulate, eventually escalating into a larger battle. A misstep with your jacket starts the evening off in a bad mood. Then before you know it, your 'feet on the end table' trick has irritated them too. Inevitably, the bickering escalates, ruining the whole evening and your chances for any form of intimacy. This is why you must take notice when something is becoming an irritant. In the case above, wouldn't it have been easy to buy a coat rack and an ottoman? Why wait for the problems to escalate? Talk it over with your partner first. Then act quickly and buy a solution, thus preventing unnecessary arguments from happening again.

Split the Difference, etc.

Splitting the difference can often be a plausible solution, especially if the area of disagreement involves something that is divisible like time or money issues. If this suggestion is too mechanical and simplistic for your particular complex romantic standoff then you might try one of the following suggestions. If both parties are agreeable, you can try a winner take all approach. For example, you can flip a coin, play a board game, draw cards or straws, or play paper rock and scissors. Another simplistic approach is alternating. For example, you compromise this time, then your partner compromises the next time. Or you decide where this weekend is being spent, and then your partner decides for the next weekend. Though the most successful compromises usually address the major needs of both persons, sometimes solutions to complex problems can be quite simple if everyone is willing to think outside the box.

Agree To Disagree

Never take a disagreement personally. No two people will ever agree on everything. In disagreements you must remember that finding common ground is the key to success and unity. Look for areas of agreement instead of areas where opinions differ. By acknowledging areas of agreement you keep the debate in a positive groove and this make it easier for everyone to agree to differ on other points. Don't feel like there has to be a winner and a loser. You may lose more than you gain by outright winning the argument if they are left be-riddled, disrespected, or emotional hurt. So be a good sport. Even if you have won the disagreement convincingly in your own mind, avoid the celebration dances. Be positive and offer to agree to disagree. Focusing on points of agreement makes your mate feel you respect and understand their differing position and that you believe unity as a couple is more important than an individual victory.

Mediation

Mediation can be an effective tool for couples who cannot reach agreement or continue to have repeated disputes over the same thing. The more hopeless a resolution may seem, the more likely it is that is needs to be mediated. Mediation helps couples to navigate through their conflict in a new ways by adding objective insights, clarifying boundaries and expectations, and by improving communication. Though mediation is offered as a professional service by many counselors, any person of mutual trust can act as a mediator. A friend, family member, or leader of your local church could be used as a mediator. Often times a good mediator can help you to reach an agreement without even interjecting their opinion or will on your issues. As the mediator asks questions to understand the issues and keeps the lines of communications open, often times the couple can reach their own resolution by grasping a better understanding of their mate's needs and concerns.

Chapter Seven: 20 Ways To Revitalize A Relationship

Tear Down the Walls

Revitalizing a relationship is like remodeling a home. The old walls must be removed before the new renovation can begin. Also like in remodeling, tearing down the emotion walls you have built in your relationship is a destructive and messy job. Yet it is absolutely necessary. To make the repairs in your relationship permanent and lasting the emotional walls of resentment, bitterness, and non-forgiveness that have been built over the years must be demolished completely. You cannot continue to overlook them because you are too tired or afraid of the emotional pain that will come with having to deal with these issues. The best tools for tearing down these walls are your earnest words. Don't be afraid to take action and deal with these old issues while taking responsibility for your own mistakes and faults. Your heartfelt words and sincere desire to fix your relationship may be all that your partner requires to let go and tear down some of their own emotional walls.

Tell Them What You Want

As you start this conversation, you must reiterate your love and commitment to them. It is important to be positive in your approach and reinforce your commitment to your ongoing relationship. It also wise to speak using words like I and we, so you do not come off as accusatory. It is also equally important that you don't tell them what you hate in your relationship or how they are falling short of your expectations. Only then will you be able to tell them everything you need, want, hope, and desire to improve in your relationship with them; only then will you be able to ask for their ideas and input. Discussing your relationship openly can be very awkward at first, but once a couple gets past this barrier, progress and improvement can often be made very quickly. You may be discontent and they don't know it, or they may have similar feelings and are afraid or unsure how to approach you. Though such conversations can be difficult to start, they often lead couples to greater trust and communication in the future.

Make Time To Be Together

When couples don't spend sufficient time together there is little or no chance for communication and intimacy to occur. A relationship can often become stressed due to unsaid or unfulfilled thoughts, actions, emotions, and needs. Resentments, jealousies, and other ill feelings can then even carry over and spoil the little time you do have together. Many times the solution to revitalizing your relationship is as simple as just finding quality time to be together on a more regular basis. Reviewing your priorities will help you to remove a few unnecessary distractions from your life and bring everything back into balance. By rescheduling time to be together, you can often draw closer to your mate. Just the effort and desire to find time to spend with your partner is often rewarded. Your attempt to improve your relationship will usually be recognized as an expression of your love and ongoing desire to be closer to them.

Forget Fault and Blame

When a relationship experiences difficulties, very often we want to assign fault and blame rather than focusing on ourselves or possible solutions. You can only heal your relationship once you have learned let go of fault and blame, when you have let go of past transgressions, and you are able to focus on how you can do things differently in the future. The real key to successfully fixing your relationship is in your ability to let go. Many times your need to be justified, your need to be respected, your need to be right, your need to be vindicated, your need for revenge, and your inability to move past fear will interfere with any workable solution to revitalize your relationship. Once you can let go of the past then you can truly forgive and forget as well as take the positive actions that can rejuvenate your relationship.

Sunsets and Moonlight

Sunsets and moonlight are inspiring for many explainable and unexplainable reasons. Artists, painters, poets, and couples have enjoyed such awe inspiring and mystical romance throughout the ages and have been motivated by their obvious beauty for just as long. Watching a sunset or taking a stroll in the moonlight together reduces stress. Time spent like this inevitable leads to good memories and positive moments that will re-unite a couple. Even without conversation, moments like these are powerful enough to inspire you to forget about your problems, and frequently move you to feel better almost instantly. Yet spending such slow time with your loved one often does encourage conversation and leads to additional opportunities to improve communication in your relationship. Good relationships and good memories are usually built by spending such positive moments of quality time together, so enjoy a sunset or some moonlight together soon.

Stop Blaming Your Mate

You must take responsibility for your own feeling and needs and not blame your mate for your own unhappiness. Blaming the mate for one's own unhappiness is a leading cause of relationship problems. This is why you must take responsibility for your own feelings. When angered by something your partner does, you must examine your own feelings and needs to determine if the right person is being blamed. Before confronting your loved one, you need to try and examine the situation objectively and clearly to determine if they really wronged you or if your own perceptions and needs are the real culprit. Even when they may be clearly at fault and the issue is important enough to address, verbally blaming them will seldom resolve the issue. Blame tends to be a negative and inflammatory action, so always try to resolve the true problem through constructive, pre-planned communication and conflict management techniques.

Love Coupons and IOUs

Using a word processing program to create a custom-made love coupon or IOU is a fantastic way to rekindle those strong feelings from the days of your relationship. If you lack the ability, time, or creativity to create a personalized love coupon, it is easy to find generic love coupons online. Just go to www.google.com or your favorite search engine and type the keywords LOVE COUPONS FREE PRINTABLE and you should find a great list of websites that have done all the work for you. Other good search terms include: IOU MASSAGE COUPON, IOU ROMANTIC DINNER COUPON, and IOU WEEKEND GETAWAY COUPON. The truth is, if you can think of an idea, then most likely somebody else has already done the hard part and made the coupon for you. Don't forget to add a personal touch to whatever generic coupon you choose by adding a hand written personalized message telling your special someone why you love, need, and appreciate them in your life.

Be Like a Child

You ever see two children fight one minute and play the next? Sure you have, but why are they able to do this? The answer is simple. Children think simple. They don't over-analyzing or attribute bad motives. Children are positive in nature, so they are happy and don't think too far ahead. They trust freely and hold no grudges. Children also forgive and forget easily. They don't need to blame the other or to prove themselves right. Couples with the longest lasting relationships often have these contagious yet child-like abilities. They simple trust and believe wholeheartedly in each other. They have learned to simplified things down to the one fact that is most important, they are committed to their partner through good and bad. It may sound odd, but it is true. If you can learn to behave like a child in these manners with your mate, most likely they will respond similarly to you; and you will have found one of the keys to revitalizing your relationship.

Make a Wish List

This is an especially effective technique for couples who are working together to re-vitalize their relationship. Each mate should make a list of five things that they want to do and see with their partner and five qualities, attributes, or things they want to improve in their relationship. Each mate should make their own list without the help of the other. This is important because often both people are looking for improvements in the same areas. When the lists are ultimately revealed to each other these common links and desires will help to reunite the couple. After making their lists, the couple should do the items together, while simultaneously working hard to fulfill their loved ones suggestions and requests for improving their relationship. Naturally a couple who wants to make the most of this time together should try to do things that are fun and exciting during the day light hours, yet still allow lots of opportunity for good conversation and quiet times together in the evenings.

Change Daily Routines

Changing your daily routine, trying new activities with new friends, changing your sexual routine, and finding new words and ways to tell your mate you love them are all good ways to add more excitement and intimacy to your relationship. Most importantly, do some new things together that are completely out of the ordinary for you as a couple, as new things tend to create new bonds and memories that will bind you together as a couple. Anything new will benefit your relationship, but thrilling adventures can magnify this new excitement even more. So don't be afraid to try something outrageous. If you are young enough and able to do something more daring, try a helicopter or balloon ride, scuba diving, mountain climbing, skydiving, or bungee jumping. as this will magnify your new bonds and memories exponentially. Also don't forget to change your perceptions; routine is not as bad as it first appears. Instead of viewing routine as a boring rut that you are trapped in, viewing it in a positive manner as stability will add to your sense of security.

Adjust Yourself

True happiness is a state of mind. This is why it is important for you to focus your thoughts on the positive elements in your life and relationship. Focus on what you hold dear and love about your partner. Negative thoughts normally lead to negative emotions and actions. To keep things on track, you must re-adjust yourself often to make sure you are radiating a content and positive vibe daily. The quality of your relationship and your mate's attitudes are likely to mirror your own disposition. Make sure you are giving off positive signals in both words and actions. Listen to your own words carefully for anything negative. Keep in mind that negative actions are always preceded by negative attitudes and perceptions. Try to hear what your mate might be hearing, especially if they might have a negative attitude about your relationship. Make sure your body language is inviting too. To warm up your relationship be sure that your partner knows you need and want them by being open to nonsexual touching like holding hands, caressing them, stroking their hair, etc.

Weekend Getaways

The hectic pace of life, the daily to-do-lists, the pressure from work, and sometimes even the stresses created from our their children at home often leads a couple to a point where there is little time for relaxation and no time to work on keeping their relationship fresh and exciting. Escaping for a few moments of down time together is a great way to prevent couples from feeling they are getting trapped in a rut of daily routine. An occasional romantic weekend getaway together helps a couple to reconnect and reignite their passion for one another. You don't have to spend tons of money or travel far away to develop an "us against the world" attitude in your relationship. Almost anywhere in the country there is a great place close by that can provide a couple with a chance to de-stress and reunite together in an affordable setting. Bed and breakfast hotels, spa resorts, and off season tourist spots can often be wonderful spots for an inexpensive escape.

Get Physical Together

Sorry guys, but unfortunately this does not mean sexually, well at least not at first. What I am suggesting here is that you restart doing physical activities together. Biking, swimming, hiking, jogging, or going to the gym together are all good ways to begin restoring your relationship. Such shared time together will let you relax and start to reconnect on a non-sexual level. Take advantage of this time to try to communicate with your best friend on a personal level, so no talking about work or the kids. It really does not matter what physical activities you do together as such time together leads to more personal communication and non-sexual touching, and inevitably these two things often lead to closer intimacy in your relationship. If your activity together is especially rigorous, make sure to maximize your opportunity at physical contact by offering your spouse a relaxing massage or taking a shower with them whenever possible.

Fix Their Things

Have you been meaning to do those projects that your spouse has been asking about, but just too busy? Well, unfortunately, your delaying is sending them the subconscious signal that everything else in your life is more important than their immediate needs. I know life is constantly hectic and there are always more things to do in a day than there are hours, but do not forget your most important priority - the one you love. If you truly want to score points with that special person and get out of the doghouse so to speak, I recommend you call in sick tomorrow and take care of these forgotten projects. Don't be afraid to tell them of your newfound realization, that you were inadvertently ignoring your most important priority – them. Not only will your partner be surprised by your sudden turnabout, I bet you will be surprised by their reaction too. So stop procrastinating right now; let that special person know that they come first in your life by fixing their things ASAP!

Recreate a Special Memory

Studies show that emotions and memories are closely tied together. Studies also show that pleasant emotions tend to fade more slowly from our memories than unpleasant memories. Recreating what science refers to as a "flashbulb memories" with your special someone can help to stir up those old strong emotions that originally built bonds and deepened the intimacy of your relationship. Recreating such powerful memories can also help to clear out and erase less pleasant memories that now may be in the forefront of their thoughts. A flashbulb memory in your relationship might be the first time you met, your first date, the day you proposed, the first time you held your child, a romantic evening you shared, or the time you went skinny dipping together. It is difficult for me to tell you what is special to your partner, but if you first spend some time reminiscing together then you should be able to determine what memories are positive emotional triggers for your loved one.

Be the Better You

Whenever we date someone new we always attempt to display the better facets of our personality, while trying to hide our shortcomings and imperfections. This is the better you that I am encouraging you to be. The better you, the person you portray yourself to be to others is in reality the person you ideally envision yourself to be. The reality is you really wish you were this better you. And so does your partner, as this is the person they originally feel in love with. It was only later that the real you showed up and started to mess things up. So when things get bad on the home front, you must take responsibility for your own failings and try to improve yourself. By striving to actually **become** the better you, you will regain their love and respect. Not only can you find great personal satisfaction and peace of mind as you improve yourself, you also will find that your relationship will improve dramatically too. So make a commitment to yourself today and to your relationship by becoming the better you - not for an hour or day, but every day.

Increase Sexual Activity

Many times sex decreases as our displeasure with our partner increases. This can be especially true when a woman is upset with her man. If you use sex as a reward and as punishment depending on your partner's performance, you may be ultimately responsible for resentment and revenge in other areas of your relationship. Often times by just restoring sex to a relationship then the other issues become smaller and more negotiable for your partner. If you use sex as a weapon to punish your partner tonight, tomorrow they may subconsciously or even deliberately be less attentive to another of your concerns. Depriving them of sex may unknowingly be what caused a vicious cycle of decline in your relationship and sex life. On the other hand, if you willingly give them sex, hopefully they will respond to your positive actions with positive actions of their own. Remember you usually get back what you give in a relationship, so always be positive.

Flirting

You should already know how to flirt with your mate on some level, yet if you give this a little thought and effort you can appreciate even more how flirting with your loved one can be a powerful tool to make your relationship fresh and dynamic. Flirting with that special someone in your life is a great means to show them love and attention. Flirting when done properly shows your life partner that you are still interested and attracted to them. Flirting can be done in many ways. It can be as simple as smiling, whispering, or touching them gently in non-sexual ways. It can also be done in more direct manners including touching, dancing, sexual banter, sexual teasing, showing them your "assets", or even through outright seduction. Another way flirting can be done is in the form of role playing. Role playing can even be used to remind your partner of how you met if you can remember special things that were said and done during your courtship.

Go To Church Together

Church can re-vitalize your spirit, attitude, and relationship. I truly recommend you head to church, preferably as a couple. Your willingness to go to church, with or without them, to improve things at home may alone re-ignite your partner's love and trust in you. A strong belief in God often makes problems seem less significant and will help you to put small daily issues back into their proper perspective. As a belief in god is also a belief in doing good to others, church will remind you of all the necessary unselfish qualities and personal sacrifices that will benefit your relationship. The closer you are to God, the more likely you will have the qualities and insights that will benefit your relationship. A refresher course in faith will definitely unite and strengthen you as a couple. If you make an effort, I assure you God's love and wisdom will never let you fail. His guidance and outpouring of blessings will be obvious, leading your relationship back to happier times.

Marriage Counseling

Marriage counseling can help couples to identify and resolve problems through better communication. By acting as a neutral mediator, a good marriage counselor can often help couples understand the deeper root causes of existing problems without necessarily taking sides or assigning blame. Marriage counseling is most effective when a couple participates, but services are offered on an individual basis too. Please do not assume you cannot afford marriage counseling as there are many free services available to couples in need. The internet, the military, local community health clinics, your local church leaders, and even the employee services office of your own employer may offer free marriage counseling. In my most recent search online, I found dozens of places offering free service in my local area. Like other medical issues, marriage counseling is often offered at an affordable rate based on your income, thus making the service available to all in need.

Chapter Eight: 20 Ways To Improve Your Sex Life

Discuss Your Sex Life

If your marriage is stable overall and your sex life has not deteriorated for more problematic reasons such as infidelity, long lasting resentment, or some deeper more profound reasons then simply discussing your sex life openly may quickly resolve a growing issue that could potentially destroy your relationship. Daily routines, changing priorities, and the presence of children in the relationship are some of the many factors that can often cause a couple's sex life to subside or to get off track so to speak. Sometimes the solution to improving your sex life is as simple as telling your partner you need them more. You might be quite surprised to discover your partner is as anxious and willing as yourself to find the passion that once burned so intensely in your relationship. Approaching the subject may seem difficult at first, but the long term benefits of such a discussion far outweigh the momentary discomfort and awkwardness of starting such a conversation.

Forget About Orgasms

If there major problems at home, your mate may not be ready to even touch you. Since you cannot score if you have not reached third base, you must forget about orgasms and start from square one. Existing issues, bad feelings, and resentments must be resolved first. Keep in mind the success of your sex life correlates directly to the success of your relationship. To get to first base, you probably will need to discuss improving your relationship with your partner. You will also need to take responsibility for your mistakes and apologize. Getting to second base might include changing your attitude, regaining their trust and friendship, restoring communication, and making them feel unconditionally loved. Basically second base is the dating stage. Getting to third base might include improving their desire for physical intimacy by hugging, holding hands, sitting close, stroking their hand, giving massages, etc. All this might take quite some time if your relationship is on the rocks, but only then can you try to steal home plate.

Change Your Sexual Routine

We are creatures of habit and often tend to get into a sexual rut by following a routine that we know works for us. After a while sex can begin to feel routine, even boring to one or both partners. It is important to remember - sex is a form of play, and it should always be spontaneous and fun. You should never be afraid to be creative, even goofy if necessary. There are many things you can do to find that missing spark and change the game so to speak. Alter the speed of your approach, by adding more time for foreplay. Kissing new places on your partner's body can be very stimulating to your sex life. Changing the type of sex you are having can also be revitalizing. Try slow sex, fast sex, dominating sex, submissive sex, oral sex, etc. Try new positions and even new places to have sex. Change the way you talk during sex. Even if it might feel weird at first, this can be pleasing to your partner. Please your mate and they will usually try to please you back too.

Be Available

Make time to be with the person you love. Don't allow less important priorities to cause too many separations or distractions in your life. Turn off the TV, give the kids some money for the movies, or do whatever it takes to make yourself available for your partner. Look carefully at your life, and try to make ways to have private time every day that is dedicated to you and your partner. For example, you can arrange the children's sleep schedule so there is an hour left every night, or you can awake early to have a little private time each morning. Even if you don't intend to have sex daily, this private time together will build the intimacy and desire for the times when sex is wanted. If you are hoping for more sex in your relationship, then don't be afraid to ask your spouse to work with you to make more time for conversation and intimacy. Just making an effort to be available may impress your partner and get you a little affection in return.

Make Them Feel Needed

If your loved one feels appreciated and needed in other areas of your relationship, it is more likely they will try to please you in the sexual aspect too. So make sure you commend your partner for all the things you appreciate about them, as well as for their sexual efforts and the ways they please you in the bedroom. A little commendation from you today may result in twice as much effort and opportunities from them. It is human nature to try to please our loved ones, especially when are efforts are recognized and appreciated. Especially for women, sex only for the purpose of sex becomes less significant and less desirable to them. Sex may then become more like a chore or duty, as they try to meet their man's needs more out of obligation than personal desire. However; this is not necessarily the case when a man lets the woman know that he loves, adores, and needs in every aspect of his life. Communication of appreciation helps to unite the man's desire for sex with the woman's desire for an emotional connection.

Listen to Yourself

Can't figure out why he or she is moody? Listen to yourself sometime and to your body language also. Negative comments are a cancer that will destroy your sex life quickly. Your sighs, sarcasm, scoffing, little put downs, and other derogatory remarks could be the cause. Any words of derision and dissatisfaction must be avoided completely. You may think you are only venting a little or expressing yourself. Or you may think they understand and accept you for who you are, but these small words and signals you are sending may be the on and off switches to improving your sex life. Negativity always leads to some degree of resentment and ill feelings, inevitably influencing the intimacy in your relationship. On the other hand, positive and kind words are the medicine, the cure all to damaged relationships. Listen to your own words very carefully. Try to hear the worst in your words, as this may be what they are hearing. By changing your words from negative to positive, your sex life can often improve quickly.

Love Dangerously

A little legal foreplay in the elevator, stealing a kiss behind the backs of friends and family, or patting your loved one's butt when no one is looking is a good way to add a little fun and excitement to your relationship. Little moments like this will usually invoke an instant smile from your loved one and often a long lasting positive memory too. Actions such as these often create a positive psychology in your relationship as you express a constant need and passion for your partner in everyday situations. The success of your sex life is mathematically determined by adding up all the smiles and then subtracting all the tears. In successful relationships it is usually the little smiles that we create, anyway we can, that exponentially multiple the happiness and intimacy of the relationship. It is the sum total of such little moments on a daily basis that make people desire each other. So love dangerously, take desperate actions daily to make the person you love smile every day, and always be sure you create a whole lot more smiles than tears.

Lubricants

Sexual lubricants general allow for more and longer sessions of sex, while being sensual and fun at the same time. Though personal lubricants can be of benefit and pleasure to men too, women seem to have the most to gain by the use of lubricants. Many studies show that women who use lubricants during sex have significantly higher levels of personal satisfaction and less pain than those who do not. Applying lubricants does not need to be a distraction before sex. When done properly, applying the lubricants can actually be incorporated into a couple's sexual experience as a way of extending foreplay. Extended foreplay almost always increases a woman's natural lubricants and heightens her levels of sexual enjoyment and satisfaction as well, so this is a win-win situation for most women. Lubricants are generally water or silicone based, so do not be afraid to try a different type of lubricant if you have experienced sensitivities issues in the past.

Massages

When relationships start to disintegrate the first thing to go is physical intimacy. Through massage your hands can tell your partner that you love, need, and desire to please them without ever saying a word. Massages increase physical intimacies, improve communication, and can even rekindle lost sexual desire; thus playing a vital role in revitalizing your sex life. A massage will usually win their approval as massages are generally viewed as unselfish acts, especially when the massage occurs outside of the bedroom in a non-sexual setting. When trying to reconnect sexually, your timing and approach must be correct and casual. The more severe the issues are in your relationship, the more likely they will stop any physical contact if they suspect it is leading to sex. So go slowly. Exercise good judgment. Use any chance given to reconnect though personal conversation, and do not try to seduce them too quickly if there are too many issues that need to be resolved first.

Sexy Food

Food is a simple yet fun way to get your sex life out of the rut so to speak. Sexy foods can add humor and smiles to the bedroom experience, especially when added spontaneously to a bedroom encounter to the unexpected surprise of one of the participants. Though food can definitely add flavor to your bedroom, I do not recommend you try to spice up your sex in any literal type of way. The most common bedroom foods are whip cream, chocolate syrup, honey, champagne, ice cubes, and real fruits - like bananas, strawberries, raspberries and cherries. To avoid yeast infections or sensitive reactions, food should never be placed inside the vagina or inside the tip of the penis if possible. A shower immediately afterwards is also recommended. For those of you who are less than keen on oral sex but truly want to please your partner, bringing food into the bedroom is a good working solution. Placing something sweet at the base of the penis or outside the vagina can make the "begrudgingly done chore" more enjoyable for everyone involved.

Try a Blindfold and/or Handcuffs

Blindfold and handcuffs can be a fun and exciting way to create sexual tension and apprehension, thus magnifying a couple's sexual arousal and satisfaction. These items do not have to be used in an overtly sexual act. For an example, they can be used as an extreme form of foreplay. Once blindfolded, you can undress your partner very slowly while kissing and caressing them sensually. After they are completely naked, you can then begin to tease your partner by pausing before touching them in different unexpected spots. In this game you should go as slowly as possible, pausing and moving from one place on their body to another as unexpectedly as possible to increase their sexual anticipation. By intermixing soft and hard kisses with varying touches from your tongue and hands or maybe even a feather, silk glove, or sex toy; you can leave your lover guessing what unexpected pleasure is coming next. Remember, if you hope to play this game more than once you must not lose their trust. Don't do something foolish, no matter how tempting it is.

Experiment with Sex Toys

When things are going good in the bedroom then couples tend to get along better in the day time too. Sexual satisfied couples tend to be more physical, more jovial, better at communicating, and more able to overlook each other's small faults. Though I personally believe that the human tongue, lips, and fingers are the best sex toys ever invented, sex toys can also add enhancement to your sexual experiences. They can help bring back the sense of desire in long term relationships that often fall into boring and repetitive sexual routines. Sex toys can be especially good in relationships that are lacking in the area of foreplay. By increasing foreplay in your relationship you increase the chances of keep your sex life fresh and vibrant. If you and your lover can keep an open mind to new possibilities then sex toys might be a good solution for you. Even if your partner is completely objectionable to the idea of sex toys, it can be fun to chase them wildly around the room and then joke about it later together.

Instructional Lovemaking

Take turns having complete lovemaking sessions where one person gives ***detailed*** instructions, while the other partner must obey and follow all orders given. (Example: Kiss my neck. No, not there, Closer to the ear. Less tongue, more lips, Softer! Gently! Slower! etc.) The two keys to success is being very detailed in telling your partner what you like and do not like and remembering your partner's requests and instructions, as their preferences during these sessions will most likely be their preference tomorrow too. This is a fun and creative way to learn more about each other's bodies, erogenous zones, desires, and even fantasies. Many times in a relationship one or both spouses will be too shy or have a difficult time communicating what is more pleasurable and what is less pleasurable to their partner. Multiple sessions of instructional love making will help to remove this hesitation barrier and teach both parties how to maximize each other's pleasure and enjoyment of sex together.

Explore Fantasies Together

Open, honest communication will first be required before you can bring about greater satisfaction in your sex life through exploration of your fantasies. A good fantasy does not necessarily have to be overtly sexual, and for the sake of continued happiness in your relationship definitely should not involve other people. I believe bringing other people into your fantasies can only lead to greater insecurities, not greater sexual satisfaction. An acceptable fantasy could be romantic, seductive, charming, old-fashioned, or maybe a scene from some old movie you have watched a 100 times. It could involve dirty talking, sex toys, a spanking, or anything else that is agreeable to both parties. A good fantasy should complement both lovers, and it should not require either person to do something that is illegal or outside their normal moral boundaries. When done properly, fantasy exploration can improve communication and trust. It can give an energetic boost to your love life by adding spice and flavor to your bedroom without endangering the foundations of your relationship.

Change Foreplay

Changing your foreplay and increasing the length of foreplay are two simple ways to entice your partner and create sexual anticipation. Most women need prolonged stimulation to reach full arousal and get properly lubricated. Though foreplay can be enjoyable for men too, a woman's comfort and enjoyment of sex usually has a direct correlation to the amount and quality of foreplay she receives. I once read that women fake orgasms because men fake foreplay. I think there is a lot of truth in this humor. Foreplay includes kissing, undressing, massaging, stroking, licking, and even teasing your mate. Kissing is an especially important form of foreplay for women. Don't just kiss their lips, explore their entire body. Take your time and don't miss too many spots. You can improve the quality of foreplay by learning your partner's erogenous zones and preferences. There are tons of articles on this subject, so do your homework. A P.H.D. in Foreplay will keep your relationship and sex life vibrant.

Sexy Board Games

Adult board games can be great for relationship building and creating intimacy, especially when both partners have a similar desire to re-ignite the flame in their sex life. It is amazing how many different sexual board games there are on the market today. Almost every famous game has been sexually twisted or perverted to add fun and flavor to your bedroom. If you are too shy or too conservative to buy them locally, it is quite easy to buy them anonymously online. Even non sexual board games that you have at home can often be used for creating excitement in your bedroom. Strip poker, naked twister, strip scrabble can all be played with the conventional board game or cards by creating your own rules. The rules of spin the bottle, quarters, paper/rock/scissors, and most other games can also easily be altered to create a game that is fun and acceptable to both partners. So be creative, have some fun and excitement while taking your favorite game to a different level in your bedroom.

Music and Mood

Sex is a state of mind, not just two body parts interconnecting. Routine behavior is seldom sexually stimulating, so it is important to get your loved one in the right mood. For a direct approach one can dress sexy and serve a candle lit dinner. Yet there are many subtle ways to stimulate your mate's senses and mood too. A good start to a private evening usually requires leaving the TV off. Some soft background music will usually allow for some good conversation, humor, and smiles. Gentle lighting can help create a relaxed mood. Perfume and cologne can be lightly used so you can unknowingly stimulate their attraction to you through their sense of smell. Dressing appropriately and taking of your dirty socks or curlers and face mask will make you visually more attractive and avoid pet peeves that can be distracting from your evening's mission. Being in such a relaxed and happy environment will usually help to create the positive psychology that leads to sexual stimulation and the silk sheets that you have prepared in the bedroom.

Be Seductive

Most people think of seduction as a woman's sport but the reality is that men can be seductive too. There are many things you can change momentarily or permanently to make yourself a better seducer. The way and timing of your touch, your posture, the way you stand, how you hold your partner, the tone and depth of your voice, your choice of words and when you pause, your body language, your cologne or perfume, how and when you make eye contact can all be changed to make you more desirable. If you think a little seduction might be helpful to your relationship don't be afraid to read a few articles on the subject. You will be quite surprised at the power and control you will discover in this sexual art form. Especially in relationships where people think they know everything about their partner, making a few changes in how you interact with them can be quite effective. Taking a new and fresh approach may re-awaken your partner's interest in you.

Reminisce Together

Old memories can frequently stir up old feelings. Reminiscing can often rekindle those forgotten feelings that were present when you first fell in love and bring closer to your mate today. So do not be afraid to start a conversation and talk about the early days of your relationship and sex life. Remind your loved one of the "good old days", those "glory days", while telling them what you love and miss most about those special times. Most likely they remember and appreciate the very same things. When a couple starts reminiscing together one thing usually leads to another. For example, discussing a memory about holding hands down by the river will probably lead to holding hands on the couch today, or reminiscing about your first kiss will most likely lead to an attempt to re-enact that first kiss. Hopefully one good spark from a memory in your past can help to re-inflame the passion in your love life today, while creating another important and cherished memory for the future.

Take a Bubble Bath Together

Though I titled this *Take a Bubble Bath Together* the theme I am pushing here is to do something exciting and physical together. It could be a bubble bath, skinny dipping, body paints, strip scrabble, or a massage with just way too much oil. Such activities as these are likely to break the routine in which you find your sex life, Sharing such outrageous moments of pleasure together are very likely to remind your loved one of other good times and activities that you shared at the beginning of your relationship. Bringing such good memories to the forefront of their mind often helps to rebuild and refortify your bonds with them. By making your physical activities together fresh and adventurous you can often make things new and more vibrant in the bedroom. Whatever you decide to do, have fun and laugh while enjoying a little physical contact. The more fun and spontaneous the moment, the more likely you are to achieve the positive result you are seeking.

Chapter Nine: The Keys To Happiness Are Within You

If you hug someone they will hug you back, if you slap someone they will slap you back. This is our nature as human beings. This same principle applies to your relationship. Thus I challenge each reader to improve themselves and their interactions with the people they love most. I sincerely believe if you make a positive effort to improve yourself and your relationship then your mate will most likely follow your example. The truth is they do not even have to know you are trying to improve the relationship. If you take positive actions in your daily interactions with others, they will instinctively respond in an equally positive manner towards you.

In writing this book I have presented 199 ways can you improve your relationships. Please note clearly, I said ways *you* can improve your relationships. The emphasis is on you for several reasons. First, you obviously feel your relationship needs improvement or most likely you would not be reading my book. Second, someone has to take the first positive steps to improve the relationship, so why not you? Third and most importantly, the emphasis is on you is because you share an equal portion of the blame for the current state of your relationship.

Unfortunately in most relationships people tend to only see the shortcomings in their partners and not in themselves. Yet realistically the blame is most often shared equally by both parties. When relationships are new, couples are usually on their best behavior and their attitude is fresh and positive. When relationships are ending, the situation is completely reversed. The real people and all their flaws have been completely exposed, and the attitude and perceptions of both mates have deteriorated significantly in many ways. Almost always, both mates have sub-consciously been drawn into a negative downdraft of tit for tat emotional warfare.

Take a moment and reflect on your current relationship or your last relationship if you are currently single. When you first started dating, did you interact differently with your mate? Were you more attentive? Were you more sexual? Were you more giving of your time and energy? Were you more generous financially? Did you cook more? Did you nag less? Did you fart less? Were your words kinder? Were your expectations and demands less? And most importantly was your attitude substantially more positive in general? If your relationship is on the rocks, then you have probably noticed major shifts in attitudes in many of these areas of your relations. Yet the real solution to your problem is in the last question, as a major change in the attitude of either party can substantially improve the relationship.

I like to view relationships like two birds in flight. A new relationship is like two young birds that learn to fly together for the first time. It is fun and exciting, fresh and new. They are experiencing new and wondrous adventures together, as they help each other to soar to new heights. It seems like they can conquer the world together. There are no words that can describe the marvelous feelings and sensations of that first flight together.

A long term relationship is these same two birds a few years later, flying together south for the winter. They have already soared to great heights together, but it can often be difficult to maintain this height for the long trip ahead. Yet it can be done successfully with a lot of hard work and effort. There will be times when the flight is easy and the wind is behind them, and there will be more difficult times when the Jetstream is against them and they are passing through stormy weather together. Yet ultimately if these two birds remain united in purpose they can successfully lead their family to a safe haven to enjoy their winter together.

A relationship that is on the decline is these same two birds flying in descending circles. First one bird tires a little and then begins to circle lower; then the other bird follows their example but descends even lower than their mate just did. This negative pattern repeats itself over and over, until finally the birds land on the rocks below.

The truth is you can stop this negative cycle of decline when it starts to occur in your life. Your relationship does not need to spiral downward all the way to the rocks. If your attitude improves and you take to positive flight, most likely your loved one will instinctively follow your lead. Once again your relationship can take flight to new heights and to new adventures. Your mate does not even need to be aware that you are on a crusade to improve your relationship. The positive attitude and fresh energy you bring to the relationship will usually lead your mate to follow your lead instinctively.

As I stated earlier, if you hug someone they will hug you back; if you slap someone they will slap you back.

So how can you find the inner strength for this new and fresh attitude that you will need to improve your relationship, especially if your spouse is not participating directly in the process? First and foremost, you must take responsibility for your own actions. If your relationship has been spirally slowly downward for some time, then you must take personal responsibility for your own declining attitude and perceptions. By keeping in mind that each mistake you made along the way has contributed to the overall decline in your relationship, it becomes easier to forgive and overlook the similar shortcomings of your partner. This will allow you to forgive them more completely. Only then can you look at your mate in a new light and understand how their deficiencies are so similar to your own. Only then can your own perception improve significantly in a positive manner. Only then will you be able to break down any ill feelings, grudges, and emotional walls that are still lingering in your heart. Only then can you move forward in your relationship with a fresh attitude and a positive spirit.

The truth of the matter is your happiness can only be found in your own mind, heart, and attitude. There really is very little your life partner can do or say that is going to change your attitude and perceptions of your relationship. Your special someone could be the perfect mate in the eyes of the world, but if you perceive them as lacking in some regards then you will find yourself unhappy and lacking satisfaction. On the other hand, if you have the mental fortitude to think positive and overlook their faults, even a partner lacking in many regards can be acceptable. Thus, the keys to happiness are truly within you and your own perceptions.

I believe we are created in the image of our maker, thus self-understanding is a step towards godliness. The better you understand yourself and your own attitudes and perceptions the better you will be able to interact in a loving manner with that special someone in your life. So don't blame them every time something goes wrong in your relationship. First you must take a deep and honest look at yourself, your own perceptions, your own attitude, and even your own negativity and shortcomings. You must ask yourself if the things they are doing are just a natural human reaction to your own shortcomings. You must also ask yourself if the things that they are doing to upset you are worth the price of unhappiness you are feeling. For example, are you prepared to get a divorce or fight endlessly over the toilet seat being left up? Or would changing your attitude and perception of this problem be a better resolution? Through my own life experience and self-examinations I have discovered that more often than not a fairly large share of most day to day problems lie within me and/or my own perceptions of the situation.

When problems occur we should also ask ourselves if the real root problem is a byproduct of our own actions and shortcomings. Is the negativity we perceive in our mate a reaction to our own shortcomings, instead of an action initiated by them? Examples of these types of situations might be a wife who is withholding sex from her husband or a man who is being too controlling.

Though problems are not always so serious and obvious to see as these last two examples, taking an honest and deep look at yourself can often change your perception. Many times we are upset by the little things more than we should be. If you cannot find a truly major fault with your mate and you cannot find an obvious fault with yourself, then you need to examine the situation to make sure you are not over-reacting or blowing small problems out of proportion. Is the toilet seat really the issue or are your perceptions causing you to overreact on a daily basis? Is your attitude just negative in general? Are you attributing bad motives to your mate? Or is this a struggle for power and control? Do you feel there is a lack of concern on their part? Is there really a lack of concern on their part? Do you do similar but different things to your mate? For example, do you often leave the cupboard door open? Can you just accept this as a simple fault and let it go?

By asking yourself a series of such questions, you can often discover the real root of the problems, as well as the solution. A small change in your own outlook and attitude may be all that is required to rectify the problem. If you determine that there is another larger issue behind the toilet seat, then you need to address that issue constructively. Yelling, screaming, and fighting repeatedly about the toilet seat will not resolve a power struggle issue or your ill feelings about a lack of concern. Even when the problem is not you, you must take personal responsibility to determine the true problem and rectify it immediately. You must be careful not to allow your ill feelings to spill over into other issues that may exist in your relationship.

The reality is that most couples cannot pinpoint when things started going wrong. A good feeling relationship seems to have just soured as time went by is what I hear so often. Thus I have come to believe that most relationships deteriorate over time more often because of a combination of small actions and attitudes than because of any particularly large problem that randomly developed in the relationship. Even when a large transgression like infidelity occurs, often it is a direct result of an escalation of many smaller events that lead that person to seek physical or emotional comfort in the arms of a stranger. The truth of the matter is negative perceptions and attitudes destroy far more relationships than negative actions do. The negative actions at the end of most relationships are most frequently the byproducts of other negative energy and attitudes that have existed within the relationship for a long time.

Obviously you must want to save your relationship or you would be reading a book about 199 Ways to a Quick and Easy Divorce. So now the time has come for you to take *positive* action. Start your relationship over with a new and fresh approach today. Be the better you. Understand yourself and at times your own negative perceptions. Understand your own shortcomings and faults, so you can overlook your mate's more easily. Tear down any emotional walls that you have built. Be like the child I mentioned earlier in the book; always forgive and forget completely. Don't over analyze or attribute bad motives too quickly to your loved one. Keep things simple and positive, and don't allow any new emotional walls to come between you and your life partner. Then and only then can you move forward with the mental fortitude and resolve that you can make your relationship better.

I want to wish everyone happiness and success in the future. I hope that you can find the same degree of contentment that God has granted me. Though God plays a significant role in my life, I tried to write this book mostly from a non-religious viewpoint, even though 90 percent of the suggestions found in this book can be found in the scriptures too. Yet in closing I find myself compelled to exhort you to consider bringing God into your relationship in some form. When a couple brings God into their relationship they are united by something greater than themselves. I truly believe that only he can help guide and strengthen us as individuals and as couples to keep our perspective focused on things that are more important than ourselves, such as our relationships and families. The more you can see and understand his true love, the better you can understand your own faults and shortcomings, the better you can forgive, and more you can remain positive and up building in your relationship. I will be praying for you and for your loved ones. I sincerely pray that God will bless you and all your efforts to improve your relationship.

"

Chapter Ten: Meaningful Quotes About Life and Love

There's one sad truth in life I've found

While journeying east and west

The only folks we really wound

Are those we love the best.

We flatter those we scarcely know,

We please the fleeting guest,

And deal full many a thoughtless blow

To those who love us best.

Ella Wheeler Wilcox

Good relationships don't just happen; they take time, patience and two people who truly want to work to be together. - Anonymous

Be polite to all, but intimate with few. - Thomas Jefferson

Keep your eyes wide open before marriage, half shut afterwards. - Benjamin Franklin

Don't smother each other. No one can grow in the shade. - Leo Buscaglia

Too often we underestimate the power of a touch, a smile, a kind word, a listening ear, an honest compliment, or the smallest act of caring, all of which have the potential to turn a life around. - Leo Buscaglia

The family. We are a strange little band of characters trudging through life sharing diseases and toothpaste, coveting one another's desserts, hiding shampoo, locking each other out of our rooms, inflicting pain and kissing to heal it in the same instant, loving, laughing, defending, and trying to figure out the common thread that bound us all together. - Erma Bombeck

You know you're in love when you can't fall asleep because reality is finally better than your dreams. - Dr. Seuss

You come to love not by finding the perfect person, but by seeing an imperfect person perfectly. – Sam Keen

Most folks are about as happy as they make their minds up to be. – Abraham Lincoln

Happiness is an attitude. We either make ourselves miserable or happy and strong. The amount of work is the same. - Francesca Reigler

Love is friendship set on fire. - Jeremy Taylor

Problems in relationship occur because each person is concentrating on what is missing in the other person. - Wayne Dyer

There is more hunger for love and appreciation in this world than for bread - Mother Teresa

The best and most beautiful things in the earth cannot be seen or even touched. They must be felt with the heart. - Helen Keller

Love is an ideal thing, marriage a real thing; a confusion of the real with the ideal never goes unpunished. - Johann Wolfgang von Goethe

Don't ever mistake my silence for ignorance, my calmness for acceptance, or my kindness for weakness. - Carson Kolhoff

The way to love anything is to realize that it might be lost. - Gilbert Keith Chesterton

Pride only breeds quarrels, but wisdom is found in those who take advice. – Proverbs 13:10

A man of knowledge uses words with restraint, and a man of understanding is even-tempered. Even a fool is thought wise if he keeps silent, and discerning if he holds his tongue. – Proverbs 17:27-28

Don't rush into any kind of relationship. Work on yourself. Feel yourself, experience yourself and love yourself. Do this first and you will soon attract that special loving other. - Russ Von Hoelsche

People are lonely because they build walls instead of bridges. - Joseph F. Newton

To love is to place our happiness in the happiness of another. - G.W. Von Leibnitz

In those whom I like, I can find no common denominator; in those whom I love I can: they all make me laugh. - W. H. Auden

Whenever you're in conflict with someone, there is one factor that can make the difference between damaging your relationship and deepening it. That factor is attitude. – William James

The most desired gift of love is not diamonds or roses or chocolates. It is focused attention. - Richard Warren

Love is patient, love is kind. It does not envy, it does not boast, it is not proud. It does not dishonor others, it is not self-seeking, it is not easily angered, it keeps no records of wrongs. Love does not delight in evil but rejoices with the truth. It always protects, always trusts, always hopes, always perseveres. Love never fails. – 1 Corinthians 13:4-8 NIV

Chapter Eleven: Funny Quotes About Relationships

Most of the quotes in the beginning of this chapter have some element of truth to the humor. As you reach the end of this section I have included some quotes and one-liners that are included purely for your amusement only. Enjoy!!!

More marriages might survive if the partners realized that sometimes the better comes after the worse. – Doug Larsen

Love is blind, but marriage restores its sight. - George Lichtenberg

I love being married. It's so great to find that one special person you want to annoy for the rest of your life. – Rita Rudner

Sometimes I wonder if men and women really suit each other. Perhaps they should live next door and just visit now and then. - Katherine Hepburn

All marriages are happy. It is the living together afterwards that causes all the problems. - Raymond Hull

You meet someone and you're sure you were lovers in a past life. After two weeks with them, you realize why you haven't kept in touch for the last two thousand years. - Al Cleathen

Someone once asked me why women don't gamble as much as men do and I gave the commonsensical reply that we don't have as much money. That was a true but incomplete answer. In fact, women's total instinct for gambling is satisfied by marriage. – Gloria Steinem

The secret of a successful marriage is not to be at home too much. - Colin Chapman

As to marriage or celibacy, let a man take which course he will, he will be sure to repent. - Socrates

Never feel remorse for what you have thought about your wife, she has thought much worse things about you. – Jean Rostand, *Le Mariage*

I have learned that only two things are necessary to keep one's wife happy. First, let her think she's having her own way. And second, let her have it. – Lyndon B Johnson

Marriage is neither heaven nor hell, it is simply purgatory. – Abraham Lincoln

Marriage is the alliance of two people, one of whom never remembers birthdays and the other who never forgets them. - Ogden Nash

The difference between being in a relationship and being in prison is that in prisons they let you play softball on weekends. - Bobby Kelton

Life is a sexually transmitted disease and the mortality rate is 100 percent. - R.D. Laing

A positive attitude will not solve all your problems, but it will annoy enough people to make it worth the effort. - Herm Albright

My advice to you is get married: if you find a good wife you'll be happy; if not, you'll become a philosopher. - Socrates

Relationships give us a reason to live. Revenge. - Ronny Shakes

If you want loyalty – get a dog. If you want loyalty and attention - get a smart dog. - Grant Fairley

When a man goes on a date he wonders if he is going to get lucky. A woman already knows. - Frederick Ryder

A good marriage would be between a blind wife and a deaf husband. – Michel de Montaigne

Love is blind, but marriage restores its sight. - George Lichtenberg

A good wife always forgives her husband when she's wrong. – Milton Berle

All men make mistakes, but married men find out about them sooner. – Red Skeleton

Marriage is a fine institution – but I am not ready for an institution. - Mae West

I never married because there was no need. I have three pets at home which answer the same purpose as a husband. I have a dog which growls every morning, a parrot which swears all afternoon and a cat that comes home late at night. - Marie Corelli

The big difference between sex for money and sex for free is that sex for money costs less. - Brendan Francis

I've had bad luck with both my wives. The first one left me and the second one didn't. - Patrick Murray

I haven't spoken to my wife in years. I did not want to interrupt her. - Rodney Dangerfield

I was married by a judge, I should have asked for a jury. - Groucho Marx

My wife and I were happy for twenty years… then we met. - Rodney Dangerfield

If you want to read about love and marriage, you've got to buy two separate books – Alan King

Do you know what it means to come home at night to a woman who'll give you a little love, a little affection, a little tenderness? It means you're in the wrong house, that's what it means. – Henny Youngman

Ah, yes, divorce… from the Latin word meaning to rip out a man's genital through his wallet. – Robin Williams

A married man should forget his mistakes, no use two people remembering the same thing. - Duane Dewel

If we take matrimony at its lowest, we regard it as a sort of friendship recognized by the police. – Robert Louis Stevenson

The secret of a happy marriage remains a secret. – Henny Youngman

A Necessary Disclaimer

First and foremost, I want to state clearly that I am not a trained or licensed professional. I am not a trained or licensed doctor, psychologist, family counselor, or anything similar. Though I personally believe that the suggestions and advice I offer in this book can help the vast majority of my readers improve their own relationships, I make no claims or guarantees that the information provided in this book will be of any benefit to you and/or your relationships. I strongly recommend that anyone having serious issues in their own lives or relationships seek professional counseling whether it is from their own doctor, family therapist, psychologist, or a member of their religious community.

All the advice, information, techniques, suggestions and/or anything else that I offer in this book are provided for informational and entertainment purposes only. I would hope that through self-reflection and self-analysis my readers can determine for themselves which ideas and suggestions can improve their own specific circumstances and relationships. Though the advice I offer is usually supported by one or more so-called experts, I make no claims that any of my advice will be of benefit to you or your relationships specifically. I am providing this information to my readers with the expectation that my readers will be able to draw their own conclusions about which advice might be of benefit to themselves and their relationships. Since no two situations or relationships are the same, my readers must assume the responsibility for all consequences that occur by applying my advice to their own specific lives and circumstances. Again I strongly advise all my readers to consult with their own licensed and trained professional family counselor or doctor if they have any doubts about applying any of the techniques, information, and/or suggestions in this book to their own specific lives and relationships. Therefore the reader of this material must assume all responsibility for any decisions, actions, and/or non-actions they take or do not take.

Printed in Great Britain
by Amazon.co.uk, Ltd.,
Marston Gate.